Splashes of God-light

Splashes of God-light

Editors:
Terence Copley, Catherine Bowness, Heather Savini, Sarah Lane

BIBLE SOCIETY

BRITISH AND FOREIGN BIBLE SOCIETY
Stonehill Green, Westlea, SWINDON SN5 7DG

A catalogue record for this book is available from the British Library
ISBN 0564 040568

Designed and typeset by British and Foreign Bible Society Production
Services Department. The text is set in Swift Xpert New and Gill Sans

Printed in Great Britain by Biddles Ltd, Guildford, Surrey

Contents

Contents

The authors

Catherine Bowness

Catherine Bowness is Co-director of the Biblos Project and a senior lecturer in Religious Education. She also researches and performs historical dance and drama.

Douglas Charing

Douglas Charing is Founder-director of the Jewish Education Bureau and author of a number of books on Judaism used in British schools. He visits schools throughout the United Kingdom, providing a resource on Jewish topics.

Dan Cohn-Sherbok

Rabbi Professor Dan Cohn-Sherbok has taught theology at the University of Kent, Canterbury, and is Professor of Judaism at the University of Wales and Visiting Professor of Inter-Faith Dialogue at Middlesex University. He is the author of over thirty books dealing with various aspects of Judaism.

Terence Copley

Terence Copley taught RE in schools in Cambridgeshire, Staffordshire, and Derbyshire and is currently Professor of Religious Education at the University of Exeter. A Quaker, he is the author of more than twenty-five books for teachers and children and is Co-director of the Biblos Project.

Trevor Dennis

Trevor Dennis taught Old Testament Studies at Salisbury and Wells Theological College before moving to Chester Cathedral where he is Canon Chancellor. He sometimes preaches through storytelling and has two collections of his stories published, *Speaking of God* and *Imagining God*. He has also written two books on the Old Testament and has another in progress.

Monica Furlong

Monica Furlong has worked as a feature writer in Fleet Street, as a radio producer for the BBC, and as a freelance author. Her many books include adult and children's novels, biographies, and writing on contemplative Christianity. She is a founder-member of the St Hilda Community, which is concerned with the status and ministry of women in the churches.

Kathy Galloway

Kathy Galloway is a theologian and writer. She is a member of the Iona Community and editor of its magazine, *Coracle*. She is author of a number of books of theology and poetry. She has three teenage children and works with local churches and groups, encouraging theology in the community.

Frank Gent

Aged 47, father of three, Frank Gent is a Museum Education Officer in Exeter and an active member of the Exeter Synagogue, generally functioning as a lay minister.

John M Hull

John M Hull is Professor of Religious Education in the University of Birmingham. His most recent book is *On Sight and Insight: A Journey into the World of Blindness*.

Maurice Lynch

Formerly Director of the BFSS National Religious Education Centre at Brunel University, Maurice Lynch is well known for his skills as a storyteller and his interest in the use of story for Religious Education. His publications include *Tell Me a Story* and *Creation Stories*.

Christopher Herbert

Christopher Herbert trained as a teacher and has been a curate, RE Adviser, Diocesan Director of Education, parish priest, Archdeacon, and is now the Bishop of St Albans. He is married with two grown-up children.

Anthony Phillips

Anthony Phillips has recently retired as Headmaster of The King's School, Canterbury. Before that, he was Dean and Chaplain of Trinity Hall, Cambridge and Chaplain of St John's College, Oxford.

Fay Sampson

Fay Sampson writes fiction for children and adults, ranging from ancient myths to the near-future. A particular interest is the Celtic Church. She enjoys researching settings for books and hill-walking.

Heather Savini

Heather Savini is a Research Associate for the Biblos Project and part-time Religious Education lecturer at Exeter University. Her teaching career has been spent in Britain, Sierra Leone, and Italy. Until recently she was Deputy Head at Torquay Grammar School for Girls.

Sister Margaret Shepherd nds

Sister Margaret Shepherd is a member of the Sisters of Sion, a Roman Catholic congregation with the special task of promoting good relations between Christians and Jews. She is Deputy Director of The Council of Christians and Jews, a national organization which brings together the Christian and Jewish communities to work for mutual respect, understanding and goodwill.

Elaine Storkey

Elaine Storkey is Director of the Institute for Contemporary Christianity, a lecturer in Theology at King's College London, a member of the General Synod of the Church of England and a council member of Forum for the Future. She is a speaker, broadcaster, and author of several books, including *The Search for Intimacy*.

Frank Topping

Frank Topping is a Methodist minister and a well-known writer, performer and broadcaster.

Alan Unterman

Minister of the Yeshurun Synagogue (Modern Orthodox), Gatley, Cheshire, Alan Unterman is a part-time lecturer in Comparative Religion at the University of Manchester. He is author of books on Jewish faith, art, and literature.

Frances Young

Frances Young teaches theology at the University of Birmingham, where she is Dean of the Faculty of Arts. She is also an ordained minister of the Methodist Church.

Introduction

Terence Copley,
Catherine Bowness,
Heather Savini,
Sarah Lane

The power of story

Stories are part of our heritage. They have been bequeathed to us by that enduring but age-old art of storytelling. Today there are professional storytellers, as indeed there were wandering bards centuries ago. There is also the television set, the professional storyteller in most modern homes. We are provided, as were our ancestors, with stories to worry us, shock us, comfort us, and make us laugh.

Throughout the generations, parents, grandparents, and teachers have been storytellers, using traditional tales to reveal to the younger generations how human beings should or should not behave, how they should treat others, and how history has unfolded over the centuries. Sometimes the stories are pleasant and have happy endings, but sometimes they do not: people die, suffer hardship, or perform wicked deeds. Whatever they contain, stories are potentially powerful. They give meaning to life, attempting to make sense of its puzzles. They affect emotions and behaviour. They contain truths about human nature and the world. They have lessons to teach. The listeners are invited to share in the adventures of the characters, to identify with them, or perhaps make judgements upon them.

Oral storytelling has often preserved stories from ancient time. Indeed, many of the stories in the biblical tradition survived because they were told and retold to each generation. Jewish Midrash, Christian medieval mystery plays, and the stained glass windows in ancient churches bear witness to

Jewish and Christian desire to perpetuate and share the central stories on which the faiths are based.

The Bible itself deals with story. On one level this presents an ambiguity for, as well as meaning something which carries truth and meaning ("my story"; "the story of God's people", and so on), "story" nowadays can mean something substantially untrue ("You're telling me a story"). It is in the former sense that we chose to explore story in the Bible.

Story in the faith communities and in religious education

Religions have always appreciated the power of narrative to convey their understanding of truth. Story is indeed the source of all theology. It unites the inner and outer worlds, linking human beings to their past and handing something on to those who will live in the future. Story is also at the very heart of education for it utilizes that most powerful tool, the human imagination. The Biblos team, with a major interest in the processes of education for both young and old and a belief that religious faith is still of vital importance within the lives of many human beings, is researching the ways by which Jews and Christians are preserving and handing on biblical material in an age of technology.

During the course of our research on teaching the Bible, members of the Biblos team have had many conversations with teachers, students, and members of faith communities. The most common worry about biblical story that schoolteachers identify is that they do not know their way around the Bible and therefore find it difficult to select passages to share with students. Perhaps it is not surprising then that the most common complaint from pupils is that the same old stories are told over and over again regardless of the age of the audience. The Good Samaritan is a good story but it may be told ad nauseam, unmindful of how often the audience has heard it, whilst other equally good stories are neglected. A much wider and more challenging repertoire could be offered, but teachers need help to identify suitable selections.

Members of faith communities are often more confident in finding their way around their sacred texts but have told us that they are always looking for new ways to interest young people in the traditional tales. They want to pass on the stories in contemporary language, which is easier for modern generations to understand, but at the same time wish to remain true to the integrity of their traditional beliefs and values. The essential meaning of a story should remain the same even though the language is new.

This anthology

With this in mind, the Biblos team contacted practising members of a wide variety of faith communities, both Jewish and Christian, who work in pastoral, theological, and educational fields, or who have a role in the media, or earn their living as writers. We asked them to select a biblical passage and retell it for an all-age audience. (Some have done this for more than one related passage.) Finally, we asked them to tell us why they had chosen this section, why they feel the story is significant, and to comment on what it has to say to us. We present their comments in different type.

Some of the stories may be more familiar than others and we hope that readers will enjoy reading them together with the writers' commentary. One or two passages are not Bible "stories", for example, Psalm 23, but are included because they form part of the Bible's story or the wider story of God and the relationship between humanity and divinity. Some of our writers have followed the biblical text quite closely, whilst others have interpreted their passage more freely, but all have aimed to be faithful to the spirit of the text. To aid further exploration of the biblical passages, Bible references together with bracketed references for parallel passages are supplied at the start of each story.

We have arranged the stories in three sections – Vulnerability, Encounter, and Destiny – in order to express the ways in which vulnerable people in the Bible encounter God and find their destinies changed. These themes are threaded throughout the Bible and have proved very effective in our approach to biblical work with young people.

God plays a major part in the stories. That was why religious believers handed them down in the first place. The Biblos team believe this to be most important. It is a distortion to reduce biblical material to a simple collection of humanistic moral tales for they are more than this. They contain moral issues certainly but, for the original storytellers, they also preserve glimpses of the power of God and open up our horizons to wonder, to transformation, to reformation, and to revelation.

Suggestions for using the stories

Teachers and leaders of discussion groups select their material for a variety of reasons. We think our collection of stories will contribute, not only to the retelling of biblical story in its own right, but also to a discussion of general religious themes, perhaps as a means to introduce the meaning of a religious festival or to help people focus on the life of an important biblical character. Some of our stories could serve as an entry point for reflection on Jewish or Christian responses to issues such as racism or reaction to disability.

We suggest that wherever possible the stories are read aloud. As well as highlighting their drama, this also allows the reader to pass comment on the activity of the main characters within the story, or to answer questions which may arise.

Questions to raise

After sharing the story, the following questions may be asked of the listeners:

- Where does the story take place?
- Who encounters who in the story?
- Does God take part in the encounter?
- Is anyone or anything changed by the events in the story?

The teacher or leader may then wish to draw out the roles played both by God and by human beings within the passage. The listeners could be encouraged to suggest what the story might reveal about human nature or what they think it teaches religious believers about their relationship with God.

Using our imagination

Some of the stories lend themselves to dramatic presentation, for example, that of Shiphrah and Puah (in "Israel is born – and saved by a joke!"); others to quiet reflection or creative writing, for example, Elijah's story (in "Elijah on the mountain of the Lord").

After hearing some of the more reflective stories, the listeners could perhaps write a poem or a letter from the point of view of one of the central characters, for example, the prophet in "Huldah's warning", or suggest or even compose a piece of music to reflect the mood of the tale.

In almost all stories the groups could undertake activities such as:

- Consider, if this story were to be made into a film or TV series, what tune could be used in the opening sequence and as the credits roll?
- Discuss how the mood of the central characters has changed by the end of a particular story and how this could be reflected in a visual presentation. (This would be especially effective in the story of Peter and Jesus on the shore of the lake.)
- Suggest a sequel or even a "prequel" to the story in question, that is, what do you think happened next or what might have taken place just before the events described in this story? In the story of "The calf of gold", for example, what could Aaron have said or done to prevent the making of the calf of gold?

Meaning

Finally, part of the re-teller's commentary could be shared and the religious meanings in the story for Jews, Christians, and humanity in general explored.

Opening windows

The title of this book echoes the view of C S Lewis that all our storytelling is "splashes of Godlight in the dark wood of our life" (C S Carnell, *Bright Shadow of Reality: C S Lewis and the Feeling Intellect,* Eerdmans, 1974; pp 163–4). We hope that you will enjoy sharing our splashes of Godlight retold and that readers and their listeners will feel encouraged to react and interact with the stories – even become storytellers themselves – ensuring that alongside all the advantages of our age of new technology, the power of story remains a window into truth.

Vulnerability

Israel is born – and saved by a joke!

Trevor Dennis

Bible reference
Exodus 1.1–22

So Jacob and all his huge family came to live in Egypt. They had so many children, after a bit they weren't just a family any more, they were a whole people. Israel, the people of God, had been born!

The trouble was they were in the wrong place. God didn't want them in Egypt. God wanted them to live in Canaan, further to the north. He had made that quite clear to Abraham long before.

The king of Egypt – the Pharaoh they called him – he thought they were in the wrong place, too. "There are so many of them!" he shouted. "If we're not careful, they'll join our enemies and fight against us, and escape into a different country."

He was being stupid, of course. The Egyptians were far too powerful for the Israelites. But people in charge of countries don't always think straight. They sometimes get terrible fears in their heads that drive them crazy. This Pharaoh was crazy all right.

Being crazy made him cruel. He turned the Israelites into slaves, and had them working morning, noon, and night – men, women, and children – building cities for him. He was out to break them. But the more cruel he was, the more children they seemed to have. So his men drove them harder and harder, and harder and harder, till the Pharaoh thought they wouldn't be able to take any more.

But he was wrong. His plan didn't work. He had to try something else. What he came up with next was really terrible, one of the worst things anyone could try to do.

There were two midwives working in the Israelite slave camps, bringing the Israelite babies into the world. The Pharaoh hated Israelite babies, especially boy babies. They would grow into soldiers one day, he thought, Israelite soldiers, who would fight against him.

He summoned the midwives to appear before him. Their names were Shiphrah and Puah. Remember Shiphrah and Puah. They were two of the bravest people you will read about in the whole Bible. Well, the Pharaoh summoned them into his presence, and when the Pharaoh summoned you, you went.

"What does he want to see *us* for?" said Puah. "We haven't done anything wrong, have we?"

"Must be pretty serious, if he wants to see us himself," added Shiphrah.

So there they stood, in front of the Pharaoh, looking down at the floor in front of their feet, hoping he wouldn't hear their knees knocking.

The Pharaoh didn't have much to say. He didn't use their names, or even say hello. "When you're helping to deliver any of the Israelite women, see if the baby's a boy. If it is, kill him. If it's a girl, let her live."

That was all. He turned on his heel and left, while two slaves hurried Shiphrah and Puah out of the palace. They held back their tears till they were safely outside. They cried at the thought of killing babies. They cried, too, because they were so angry. Killing babies, new-born babies! *Them* killing babies! They were *midwives*! Their job was helping babies to live not die. That was what God had put them on earth to do, and they had more time for God than for that dreadful Pharaoh!

So they took no notice of the Pharaoh. They just carried on doing their work, and the Israelite women kept having lots of lovely bouncing boy babies as well as lovely bouncing girl babies.

But the Pharaoh had his spies in the slave camps. He summoned Shiphrah and Puah to his palace once again.

"Why haven't you obeyed my orders?" he roared. "I told you to kill the babies if they were boys. You've been letting them live! You haven't killed a single one! Why not?"

Shiphrah looked at Puah. She winked. Her knees weren't knocking this time. Nor were Puah's. They weren't afraid of the Pharaoh any more.

"Well, your Royal-Ever-so-Divine Highness," Shiphrah began. "It's like this. These Israelite women, they're just like animals, aren't they, Puah?"

"Yes," Puah agreed, "just like animals. They have their babies so quick! We can't get there in time, can we Shiphrah?"

"Never," Shiphrah said. "Someone comes to tell us Mrs So-and-So's having her baby, and we go rushing round as fast as we can, don't we Puah?"

"Ooh, *ever* so fast," said Puah. "But we're always too late."

"Always too late," added Shiphrah. "We get there and someone comes out and says, 'She's had it already.' And all we can do is say, 'Oh, bother!' and go on our way. Isn't that right, Puah?"

"Oh, bother," repeated Puah, and coughed loudly to hide a giggle.

And do you know what? You won't believe this! That stupid Pharaoh thought they were telling the truth! So he let them go, and when they got outside the palace they laughed so much they both got hiccups, and they had to pat each other on the back, which only made them laugh even more and get even more hiccups.

Pharaoh gave up the idea of using midwives after that. And the Israelite babies kept coming thick and fast, well *reasonably* fast, and God was really proud of Shiphrah and Puah and made sure they had families of their own and became great heroines among the Israelites.

And I wish that was the end of the story. But it wasn't, of course. Pharaoh was too crazy, too cruel. If the midwives couldn't do his dirty work, then his own people, the Egyptians, would have to do it for him. He put out a command. "Take every boy baby born to any of the Hebrew women," it said, "and throw him into the river Nile!"

You may not have heard of Shiphrah and Puah before. If you haven't, I'm not surprised. Their story may be better known among religious

Jews, but I've met plenty of Christians, even priests, who, when I mention Shiphrah and Puah, look at me with puzzled expressions on their faces. They can't remember anything about them at all, although they are in the Bible.

That's one of the reasons I like talking about this story! I like taking it out of the dark, dusty cupboard where people have left it. I like showing it to them and saying "Look at this! It's one of the brightest treasures of the Bible!" To help them see that, I have to make the story much longer, as I have done here. In the Bible it's so short. Blink, and you've missed it! So I have to use my imagination and fill in some of the detail. In some ways it's a very frightening story, and I have to help people see that. In other ways it's a very funny story, and I have to bring that out, too. I hope my version of it here will make it come alive for you.

I think Shiphrah and Puah are two of the greatest heroines of the Bible. They are ordered to do something that is so dreadful, and if they disobey, they will almost certainly be killed. But they do disobey, and simply because they put God first. And they get away with it! They trick the terrible Pharaoh and make him look a fool. They get the better of him, and because they do, God's plans for his people, the Israelites, can go forward. Most people, however old or young they are, enjoy stories of "little" people who are good getting the better of "big" people who are bad. The story of David and Goliath is another one like that.

But Shiphrah and Puah are especially important because of where their story comes in the Bible. It comes at the very start of the long story of the people of Israel. You will not find the people of Israel in the book of Genesis. You will only find their ancestors, Abraham and Sarah, Isaac and Rebekah, Jacob and his wives Rachel and Leah. Genesis is about a family, not a people. We don't hear about the people of Israel till the first chapter of the book of Exodus, and that is exactly where the story of Shiphrah and Puah comes. Together these two women save the people of Israel, God's people, from being wiped out by a wicked king. They save the ancient plans of God himself from being destroyed. What would have happened if Shiphrah and Puah had obeyed the Pharaoh's terrible orders to kill the Israelite babies? That would have been the end of Israel, the end of the story! That's what the story makes me think, anyway. That's what the story is meant to make us all think. Now you can see why I call Shiphrah and Puah two of the greatest heroines of the Bible.

And there's another reason why I chose this story. When I imagine myself being there when it was first told, if I shut my eyes, I hear women's voices. I think this story was probably first told by a woman to other women. That makes it even more interesting. Because although we have quite a lot of stories *about* women in the Bible, we don't have many stories *by* women. I think this is one of them.

The enemy of the Jews

Dan Cohn-Sherbok

Bible reference
Esther 1.1–8.17

The Jews always seem to have had a hard time. It's been so for centuries. But there is one story in the Bible which is encouraging! The Book of Esther describes the Jews' victory over their enemies. For this reason it's one of my favourite books of the Bible. Every year during the festival of Purim this narrative is read in the synagogue. Boys and girls dress up in costumes, and whenever the name of the villain in the tale, Haman, is mentioned, they stamp their feet and make a lot of noise.

This is the story: a long time ago in Persia there was a king named Ahasuerus who was married to a very stubborn queen named Vash'ti. Once when the queen was commanded to appear before the people, she refused. The king was furious and decided to get rid of her. The king's attendants told him to gather up all the beautiful maidens in the vicinity so that he could choose a new wife.

Now there was a Jew in Persia whose name was Mordecai. He had been taken away from Jerusalem as a captive, and had been guardian of his niece Esther since her parents died. Esther was very lovely, and when she was taken to the palace she won the heart of the king. But she didn't tell him she was Jewish. This is what Scripture says:

> . . . the king loved Esther more than all the other women; of all the virgins she won his favour and devotion, so that he set the royal crown on her head and made her queen instead of Vash'ti. (Esther 2.17)

Some time later, Esther's uncle Mordecai uncovered a plot to overthrow the king. He told Esther and Esther reported it to the king. Then the men who were guilty of treason were hanged. At this time King Ahasuerus promoted one of the men at the court, whose name was Haman, to a high position as his adviser. Everybody in the kingdom was ordered to bow down to Haman, but Mordecai refused.

Haman was incensed. And he resolved to kill all the Jews living in the realm. Speaking to the king, he told him what he planned. "There is a people," he said, "who are living amongst us. Their laws are different from everybody else's. They don't keep the king's laws. So it doesn't profit you to tolerate them. What you ought to do is issue a decree that they be killed."

The king gave his consent. His secretaries were summoned to give orders to get rid of all the Jews and take their possessions. But when Mordecai heard about this decree, he was horrified. He went to Esther and told her that she must save her people. So . . . the queen put on her royal robes. She stood in the inner court of the palace. And she asked her husband the king to invite Haman to dinner at the palace.

Haman was thrilled. He bragged to his friends about the invitation. "Ha," he said, "I've been invited to the palace for supper!" But even though he was delighted to receive this invitation, he was upset about Mordecai's refusal to bow down to him. "How could this fool be so stupid?" he asked himself. "I'm going to get even." Then he built a gallows for Mordecai, and said to himself: "I'll become hangman for that horrible Jew!"

Haman, however, did not succeed with these plans. When the king learned that Mordecai had previously uncovered a plot against him, he asked his attendants if Mordecai had ever been rewarded. They told him that nothing had been done. At this stage Haman entered the palace, determined to persuade the king to hang Mordecai on the gallows that he had constructed. When Haman appeared before the king, the king asked him what should be done to someone he wished to honour. Thinking that the king was referring to himself, he said:

For the man whom the king wishes to honour, let royal robes be brought, which the king has worn, and a horse that the king has ridden, with a royal crown on its head. Let the robes and the horse be handed over to one of the king's most noble officials; let him robe the man whom the king wishes to honour, and let him conduct the man on horseback through the open square of the city, proclaiming before him: "Thus shall it be done for the man whom the king wishes to honour." (Esther 6.7–9)

While Haman was enjoying a banquet at the palace, this is what was done to Mordecai without Haman knowing anything about it: Mordecai was given royal robes and rode in triumph on horseback through the city.

On the second day of the banquet, the king told Esther that he would grant any request she made. Overcome with emotion, she pleaded for her people.

"Oh, king," she said, "if you love me, save the Jewish nation."

The king was confused and asked his wife: "Who has plotted against the Jews?"

"It was Haman," she replied. "He is our greatest enemy."

Granting Esther her wish, the king had Haman hanged on the very gallows he had prepared for Mordecai. The king then requested that his secretaries write to the governors of all the provinces where the Jews lived, allowing them to defend themselves from attack.

To commemorate this victory over those who seek to destroy them, the Jewish nation has celebrated the festival of Purim from generation to generation. Every year the Book of Esther is read in the synagogue. And in so doing, Jews remind themselves that God will be with his chosen people even in the most terrible circumstances – the Jewish people must never lose hope. You can see why this tale is so important for the Jewish community. And whenever I feel miserable, I think back to these events that took place in a foreign land thousands of years ago. The story of Mordecai and Esther and King Ahasuerus reminds me that God will not abandon those who trust in him and turn to him in their despair.

Paralysis

Frances Young

Bible references
Mark 2.1–12 (Matthew 9.1–8; Luke 5.17–26); John 5.1–18

I expect you've seen people with disabilities competing in sports at the Paralympics or in the London Marathon's wheelchair race. People in wheelchairs may be "paraplegics" (that is, unable to move their legs) either because of accidents or illness, or because they were born that way. Lots of people with disabilities miss out on the opportunities the rest of us have. Just a few have the determination to make something of their lives and compete. For them it's extra hard. Life isn't a level playing field. All of us feel sometimes that it's no good trying, and we're really up against it. It's that much worse if you start with legs that don't work.

Back in the time of Jesus, 2000 years ago, there weren't any wheelchairs. People who couldn't walk were even more left out. They couldn't have jobs and often ended up as beggars. Or they just stayed at home and couldn't go out at all. So it was really surprising one day when a paralysed man literally landed at Jesus' feet.

The way it happened was like this. In Israel, a hot country with almost no rain, people would usually gather outdoors to do things together, but that day Jesus was teaching in somebody's house. The heat was so bad everyone had gone into the cool darkness inside. There were far too many people packed in. You couldn't get anywhere near.

The houses all had flat roofs, and you could get up on to them. People sometimes slept up there under the stars because at night it was cooler than inside. As the crowd listened to Jesus, some noticed there was a commotion going on over their heads. They were amazed to see light, coming first through a tiny hole, but soon through a bigger and bigger opening. Jesus kept on as if nothing was happening, until right there in front of him, there was this big blanket bundle, tied with ropes at the four corners, being let down as if held by a crane. People stepped back and it landed on the ground exactly at Jesus' feet. Curled up inside was a paralysed man, staring up at Jesus with terror in his eyes. Looking down through the hole were the faces of the four who'd carried him there on a sort of stretcher, then heaved him up on to the roof and dug out the hole to let him through.

Glancing from one to the other, Jesus quickly took in how much effort it had been for those four, how much they cared, how much they depended on him to do something to help this paralysed man. After all, Jesus was already well known as a healer, and hope had given them the energy to bring their friend or brother or neighbour – didn't matter who it was – it was the determination it took to get him there that counted. Up above, their faces were full of expectation. But down here there were eyes full of dread. Jesus looked deep into those eyes and said something quite unexpected: "Your sins are forgiven."

First there was a shocked silence, then uproar. The religious leaders started muttering. Some were shouting:

"Who do you think you are? Only God can forgive sins."

"What do you mean by this kind of talk? It's scandalous!"

"You can't claim to do what only God can do."

But Jesus kept looking into the eyes of the terrified man lying at his feet. He noticed a deep change starting to take place in him. The man's eyes had lost their hunted look. His body seemed relaxed. It seemed as though Jesus knew this was a man who hadn't been able to face life because of some terrible thing he'd done. He'd thought he could never be forgiven and he'd never be free from the shame and horror of it in this life nor the next. Jesus knew the real healing had happened already.

So he raised his eyes and glared at the source of the hubbub all around him. People began to shut up, curious about what he would do next. Then he asked a question: "Is it easier to say 'Your sins are forgiven' or to say 'Get up, take up your stretcher and walk'?"

They didn't dare answer. Jesus made sure they understood that he intended to prove they were wrong, then turning back to the paralysed man, he said "Get up, take up your stretcher and walk."

Slowly but surely the man did exactly that. Somehow, with Jesus there, he felt he could walk when he couldn't before, and so he got up and walked off into a new life. Jesus had done two things impossible for human beings – healed a disability and forgiven sins. So was he more than human?

Now they say that story happened in Capernaum. There's another story rather like it we're told happened in Jerusalem. This time the paralysed man didn't have any friends. He was lying by a pool that was supposed to be magic: after the water was disturbed – some said an angel stirred it up – the first person who got in would come out healed. So there was the man longing for a miracle. Jesus came along and said, "Do you want to be healed?"

The man started moaning about not having friends and how he could never get to the water first – it was always someone else. It wasn't fair: he was just stuck there, unable to do anything. Jesus realized this man was tied up in self-pity. All he could think about was the terrible, lonely state he was in and how no one understood or cared. He thought he couldn't do anything for himself and so he couldn't. He thought the only thing for it was to wait for a miracle that never came.

So Jesus gave him a shock. He said, "Get up, pick up your stretcher and walk." Somehow, with Jesus there, he felt he could walk when for 38 years he hadn't been able to. As he realized the compassion Jesus had for him, he found he wasn't helpless and friendless after all. He too got up and walked off into a new life.

But Jesus found himself in trouble again with the religious leaders, on this occasion because he'd "worked" on the Sabbath day, and that wasn't allowed according to the Law of God they were supposed to live by. This time Jesus said, "My Father is always working, and I too must work." He was trying to prove that if God could keep the world going on the Sabbath, then there was no reason why he shouldn't do God's work of giving people new life. When the leaders heard this, they were furious because they thought he was making himself equal to God. After this, they were determined to find a way to have him killed.

So who do you think he was? These stories prod us to answer these questions too. They show Jesus doing things that only God can do. Was he more than human, as the people who first told these stories believed? What do you think?

I suppose most people who've heard these stories have been amazed at Jesus' miracle-working power. But in recent times lots of people have started to say, "They must be like fairy stories. Paraplegics can't walk again." And people with disabilities have begun to protest against being told that if they have enough faith they will be healed. They feel they are being blamed for their disability.

But in these stories the people Jesus healed didn't have any faith. And their paralysis was something nearly all of us sometimes suffer from. They stand for human beings who are trapped into living useless lives because of things they've done wrong, or into giving up because they are full of self-pity. What Jesus did was not to wave a magic wand, or even use the magic water of the pool, but to prove that life's difficulties don't have to disable us. Jesus stimulated both men into believing they could walk after all. What is really sad is when anybody, with or without disabilities, allows life to get them down or runs away from responsibilities.

Then there's another thing. In both stories the importance of friends or helpers is obvious. When other people believe in you, it can lead to new possibilities. When no one cares there's not much hope. Sometimes we can be the helpers; at others, we need to be able to accept help and not feel we've lost our dignity or our independence. We all belong together, and it's only together that we can find out how to live a full life.

But the healings are not the main point of the stories. The stories show Jesus proving that God is involved in the ordinary ups and downs of human life. Religion sometimes gets in the way of releasing God's goodness. These stories show how Jesus, "the Son of Man", embodies God's goodness in a human being. The same goodness of God can be at work through those who follow Jesus' way.

So why did I choose these stories? Because I think stories like this challenge us to recognize how cramped and disabled our lives are much of the time. They remind us of how much we need other people and how much we can learn from people with disabilities. But, most of all, I chose them because my son was born with severe disabilities and, even though he's not cured physically, I know that God has changed our lives in ways rather like the experiences of those men with paralysis.

The calf of gold

Alan Unterman

Bible reference
Exodus 32.1–29

About three and a half thousand years ago, long before the age of the Greeks or the Romans, the children of Israel were suffering as slaves in Egypt and cried out to the Lord for help. God responded to their prayers and looked for someone he could send to convince the Pharaoh, the Egyptian king, to let the Israelites go and who could lead them through the desert to the Promised Land.

He chose Moses, an Israelite of the tribe of Levi, as his messenger because Moses had grown up in one of the royal palaces of Egypt. Having been adopted by the Pharaoh's daughter, Moses understood the inner workings of the Egyptian court. Moses had also shown his courage by killing an Egyptian who was mistreating some Hebrew slaves. At the time that God called Moses, he was a shepherd, and so he knew what it meant to be the leader of a flock.

Moses, however, was at first very reluctant to go and plead the cause of the Israelites because he stuttered. With his stammer, he doubted whether he could make an impression on the Pharaoh, who was surrounded by smooth-talking courtiers. He also knew he faced the equally difficult task of convincing the Jewish slaves themselves that they could be free men and women.

When he approached the Pharaoh, the king naturally resisted Moses' request because he was in need of the cheap labour that these slaves provided. It was only after God brought a series of disasters upon Egypt that the Pharaoh and his fellow Egyptians decided that the price they had to pay for ruling over the Israelites was too high. So thousands of ex-slaves followed Moses into the desert, on their way to the Promised Land.

While they were wandering in the wilderness, the Egyptians had a change of heart and decided to recapture them when they were held up by the waters of the Reed Sea. Fortunately for the fleeing Israelites, a miracle occurred – the sea opened and they managed to pass through on dry land. The Egyptian chariots, however, got stuck in the mud and the warriors were drowned as the waters returned.

After this miraculous escape, Moses brought the Israelites to Mount Sinai, a small mountain in the Sinai Desert. Here they were told about the Ten Commandments and taught that God wanted them to live by his laws. Moses went up to the top of the mountain to be instructed by God and he remained there for forty days and nights.

It was while Moses was away that the calf of gold was made. The people became restless when they saw that Moses did not return and seemed to have disappeared. Though they were now free people, they still had the mentality of slaves. A number of men approached Aaron, the High Priest and brother of Moses, and demanded that he make an image for them to lead them. This, after all, was what they were used to in Egypt, a culture of semi-divine images and of idols.

Aaron realized that their request was foolish but they were desperate because they felt they had been abandoned in the desert. Aaron decided to play along with them. He adopted delaying tactics by asking them to bring him the gold earrings which were worn by their wives and children. No one would really want to give up their most precious possessions, he thought, but he was wrong. The people brought their gold ornaments to him and Aaron melted them down and made them into the image of a calf.

When they saw the calf of gold the people said: "This is your god, Israel, which brought you out of the land of Egypt." Aaron still tried to delay things in the hope that Moses would return at any moment. So he declared: "Tomorrow there will be a feast to the Lord."

Well, next day Moses had still not come back and the people got up early in the morning and offered sacrifices to the idol. They then sat down to eat and drink and when they had finished they started rejoicing wildly.

God told Moses to go down from the mountain because the people that he had brought out of the land of Egypt were behaving badly: they had forsaken the way that God had commanded them and made an image of a calf which they were worshipping. God said that the people were a stiff-necked people, and he wanted to destroy them. He would then make Moses himself into a great nation.

Moses must have been very disappointed with the children of Israel. They seemed to have learned nothing from their experience of God's salvation. But instead of rushing down the mountain to blame them, Moses pleaded with God not to destroy the Israelites. He reminded God of his promise to Abraham, Isaac, and Jacob, the ancestors of the Israelites, to make their descendants into a great people who would be as many as the stars of the heaven, and to give them the Promised Land. In this way, Moses persuaded God to change his mind.

As Moses came down the mountain after this, carrying the two tablets of stone on which the Ten Commandments were written, he heard the sound of a riotous party in the Israelite camp. As he came near, he caught sight of the calf and saw the people dancing, and in his anger he threw the two tablets down and smashed them. Then he took the calf, burnt it, and mixed the resulting powder with water which he made the Israelites drink to convince them that there was nothing magical about an idol.

In order to stop the wild behaviour which was going on, Moses asked for volunteers to help him protect the teachings of the Lord. The tribe of Levi, which was Moses' own tribe, came forward and went around the camp killing those who would not calm down and would not give up the golden calf worship.

The story of the calf of gold highlights what happens when a strong leader disappears. How do people react in a situation when they are not used to making decisions for themselves? Do they just become part of a mob, desperately searching for anyone or anything to lead them, or do people rise to the occasion? While touching on the fickleness of people, the story raises questions of what true religion is all about, who is responsible for what goes wrong in society, and what qualities are expected of a real leader.

This episode has a universal message because we all suffer from a slave mentality at times and want something concrete to worship. We, too, find it very difficult to stand up for what is right when everybody around us is behaving badly or foolishly.

Obviously, the people who wanted to replace Moses with an idolatrous image were primarily to blame for what happened. They found it too hard to worship an unseen God and they abandoned themselves to a drunken orgy and idol worship.

They were also too impatient and we can sympathize with them because we also like everything instant: instant foods, instant riches that come from the lottery, instant excitement that comes from a TV, a video, or a computer game. Yet impatience is a vice. When we are too impatient for something, the impatience can spoil it all.

Was Aaron also to blame for what happened? As High Priest he was left in charge by Moses, and he should have resisted the people's demands. Perhaps he could have reminded them of all that God had done for them and of the dedication of Moses to the Israelites. Aaron clearly suffered from being a Mr Nice Guy, which is not the best recipe for leadership.

Even Moses does not emerge from the story entirely without blemish. He is shown to be a man with a very strong temper, exemplified by his smashing of the tablets of stone. Yet he was someone who overcame his disability as a stutterer and acted as a true leader. Moses put the people first and was not afraid to stand up for them even against God himself.

The message of the calf of gold is that easy solutions are not always the best ones. Living with God can demand stamina, patience, and courage. It is sometimes very difficult to hold on to our beliefs and religious ideals in a world which only values things that can be seen and felt, like money or possessions. In the end, however, people will come to realize that there is nothing magical in idols of gold.

A quiet cure

Frank Gent

Bible reference
2 Kings 5.1–19

I had to choose this story. I have been living and breathing it for almost a year, studying every word, singing it over and over again, as I taught the story to my son for his bar mitzvah. This took place on the sabbath on which we read Leviticus 13, which deals with the laws concerning leprosy in biblical times, and the story of Na'aman from the Book of Kings, chosen as the accompanying reading because it tells of a person afflicted with leprosy.

We studied the Hebrew text intensively, pronouncing every consonant and vowel exactly and carefully. We studied the phrasing and saw how the chanting reflected the meaning, and, of course, we studied the story.

Na'aman was the general in charge of the army of the king of Aram. Aram was Syria, a country which had beaten Israel and from where raids frequently took place. A successful general, Na'aman had waged war against the Israelites and inflicted defeat on them and their king, who became a vassal to the king of Aram. Indeed, a captured Israelite girl was servant to Na'aman's wife, and it was the comments she made to her mistress that changed Na'aman's life.

This is what happened. Although he was a man of power and influence, Na'aman had leprosy, a terrible, disfiguring illness. It was the Israelite servant girl who remarked that there was a prophet in Israel who could help Na'aman, even cure him of his illness. The prophet was Elisha, successor to the great Elijah, and his fame travelled with the Israelite girl to the household of Na'aman in Aram.

The hope of a cure was sufficient to encourage Na'aman to ask his master, the king of Aram, for permission to travel to the land of Israel. The king obliged with a letter of introduction, and Na'aman set out with his entourage, laden with treasures and clothes, which he intended to give as gifts to Elisha if he was cured.

When the king of Israel received the letter from the king of Aram, he panicked, not knowing how to cure Na'aman himself, and suspecting a plot to justify an attack against him. (The traditional synagogue chanting of this section reflects his agitation, as he tore his clothes in anguish.) In fact, the king of Israel had misunderstood, and the prophet Elisha told the king to stop fretting and send Na'aman to him. Na'aman went to Elisha for a cure, but when he reached Elisha's home he was met by a servant who had been sent to tell him to jump in the River Jordan seven times.

Na'aman was disgusted. The so-called prophet and miracle-worker wouldn't even come to the door and meet this great general from another, superior, country. And this was no suitable cure, jumping in the river: it lacked drama. Where was the thunderbolt, the hand of God, the flash of lightning? The Jordan is no big shot as a river, either. (When I first saw it when I went to Israel in 1979 I admit to disappointment: it's more like a stream.) Na'aman was completely unimpressed – Syrian rivers were bigger and better – and he lost his temper, refusing to try such an unglamorous remedy.

Na'aman's attendants, who had come with him, saw things differently. First they let him lose his temper, and then they let him know how high and mighty he was being in wanting a flashy cure. So Na'aman agreed to give it a try. Seven times he dipped in the Jordan, and his flesh was made whole – like that of a child, the story says. And was Na'aman grateful! He wanted to reward Elisha, but Elisha refused any gift.

Na'aman promised from now on to believe only in the God of Israel, and asked for two loads of soil to take back with him to Aram. A strange request you might think, but Na'aman felt he could only worship the God of Israel on this God's own territory, so he decided to cart some of that territory home with him. As far as he was able, Na'aman was sincere in wanting to switch his allegiance to the God of Israel, but he asked the prophet's permission to go into the temple of Rimmon, the king of Aram's god, whenever he had to do so as part of his duties. Elisha told him to go in peace, and, presumably, the permission was granted "on the nod". Na'aman wasn't ready, nor was he required, to give up everything for the God of Israel.

I like this story for a number of reasons. For example, the fact that Na'aman was able to succeed despite his disability. I like the terror of the king of Israel when he thought "Big Brother", the king of Aram, was picking on him. I like Na'aman's initial arrogance. He wanted a BIG cure, something dramatic, something memorable, to match his status. I like Na'aman's cop-out: conversion but with exclusion clauses.

Was Na'aman's leprosy the equivalent of being HIV-positive nowadays? It was an affliction with no known cause, and it was certainly viewed as a punishment by some. It didn't kill, but it often turned people into outcasts, although Na'aman's high status seems to have protected him from this.

After three millennia, it is the complete humanness of the individuals that still comes through in this story. There is the cowed king of Israel; the arrogant general; and the unpretentious prophet who treats all alike. And there is the option to "bow down in the house of Rimmon", the surprising recognition that Na'aman was not placed to give up everything and follow the prophet.

I didn't know until recently that to "bow down in the house of Rimmon" is an accepted phrase for paying lip service to something or, at worst, performing an act insincerely and dishonestly. Now that I know the phrase, I know that I too "bow down in the house of Rimmon" and we most of us do when it seems appropriate. We do it to avoid causing offence, to make someone happy, to make ourselves more acceptable to others, and because not all of us are called to be martyrs.

And is it wrong, to swallow our principles for the sake of others? To me the answer isn't clear. It all depends. It means knowing when to draw the line. When I go to a Christian service, for example, I draw the line at kneeling down, or at praying to or through Jesus, and I draw the line at singing hymns whose sentiments I cannot agree with. But I don't "make a statement": I do it quietly. Like Na'aman, who wanted to please his master the king, I want to please my friends and family.

As a Jew, there are certain things I am expected to firmly draw the line at, even to die for. What is worth dying for? My faith tells me that to save a human life just about any rule or belief can be broken, except when it involves the extreme wrongs of idolatry, unchaste acts such as incest or adultery, or murder. The reality for Jews in the past, whether in medieval Europe or the twentieth century, was that they often did pay the final price for their beliefs, but they felt that their faith was worth dying for.

The story of Na'aman's cure in the puny Jordan also has a lasting message, I think. At those times when the human race seeks its own cure from moral leprosy, although other faiths, cultures, and civilizations may have wonderful, inspiring features, there is a special source of healing in the teachings of Judaism. Judaism, like the Jordan, may seem small and insignificant, but its teachings have eternal value and importance.

My mum

Kathy Galloway

Bible references
Matthew 15.21–28 (Mark 7.24–30)

She's got a real nerve, my mum. She'd give you a red face any day! I mean, I know all teenagers think that about their parents, but my mother's seriously embarrassing! She's the kind of person who'd buy you a new dress off a market stall, and then find a tiny mark on it — no one would ever notice and you're quite happy with the dress — but, oh no, "This'll not do," she says, "I paid good money for this". And before you know what's happening, we're off, back down to the market. And I'm saying to her, "You can't take it back. This is a market. If you want the really good stuff, you have to go to the really good shops that we can't afford." But she just smiles and says, "Don't worry, I'll sort it out," and you know there's going to be an embarrassing scene. You'll just have to stand there listening, wishing the ground would swallow you up, while she argues with the stallholder and everybody stares.

It's not that she's rude — she doesn't shout — she just doesn't give up. And you don't get the better of her easily. I don't know if she's always been that way, like she's ready to take on the world. I've asked her what she was like when she was thirteen. She just laughs and says that it's too long ago to remember. I think maybe she's had to be a fighter because it's just her and me. She's raised me on her own, with no one to help her. Single mums get given a hard time.

And the other side of it is, if she wasn't like that, I wouldn't be talking to you now. But you need to know what kind of a person my mum is to understand the story. Even then, you might not understand. It happened to me . . . but I wasn't there. See what I mean about confusing? Anyway, this is what happened as far as I can tell.

It happened about a year ago. For some reason, I'd got really ill. It wasn't like having a cold or being sick because you've eaten some fruit that wasn't washed properly. It was much more scary than that. I couldn't sleep at night, and I couldn't wake up in the morning. I was cold and sweaty all at the same time. Sometimes I didn't know where I was, and then I'd get all panicky and scream and cry. I used to have terrible nightmares, and sometimes I'd wake up and find myself standing outside the house. I used to pull big handfuls of my hair out, so my head was covered in bald patches, and sometimes I'd scratch my hands so badly they'd bleed. And I couldn't eat. It was horrible.

No one could tell us what was wrong. My mum spent money we couldn't afford getting in a special doctor. All he did was give me some medicine which didn't help a bit. The neighbours began to avoid us when we went out. I think they thought I was cracking up. That's what I thought. My mum tried to stay calm, but I could tell she was getting really desperate.

Then my mum heard about this man who had come to stay in our town. No one was supposed to know, but you can't keep anything secret here. Anyway, according to the rumours, he was here because he'd upset the authorities in his own country and he needed to keep out of their way for a while.

Oh, I didn't say he was a foreigner, did I? I know it's just over the border, but it might as well be the other side of the moon. That's how big the distance between us really is. They think we're heathens because we don't have the same religion as them. I remember somebody saying the reason they take their religion so seriously is because they believe they've been chosen by God. They think no one else can really understand what God wants. I don't know about all that — after all, there might be other people who want to do what God wants, too, and how are they supposed to learn? If they're right, it seems rather hard luck on everyone else.

I suppose they look at us and think, "Oh, they'll worship anyone." They don't know what they believe. There's quite a lot of them live here, actually – but we don't mix. They live in their area and we live in ours. Even the children play separately. You just grow up with it. They call us "dogs". Well, you're not going to feel very friendly towards people after that, are you?

To get back to the man; it seems that he was actually quite different from the very holy ones. Apparently, he'd been sticking up for the poor people and preaching to big crowds, telling them that God loved all of them, and that what was in their hearts was more important than what they ate or how they said their prayers. When my mum heard that, she liked it: "At last a preacher with some sense," she said. But what really got her going was when she discovered that he'd also been healing people, including a girl about my age. That's when she said she was going to go and find him and ask him to make me better.

Normally, I would have thought, "Oh no, another embarrassing scene. She's going to go marching in disturbing someone who's trying to get away from people. He'll think she's a bad woman because she hasn't got a man with her and, anyway, she's not one of them, so why should he help her?" But this time I was too ill to know what was happening, let alone try to stop her. I just watched her set off down the road and I got more and more agitated.

I'll try and describe what happened next from what my mum's told me. In a few minutes, she reached where he was staying, and already she was feeling pretty nervous because it was in one of their areas. She'd never set foot there before. She took a deep breath, thought about me for a moment, and then she went in.

There were some men there — his friends, I think. (It must have been awful, all of them staring at her.) I asked her how she knew which one was him. "I just knew," she said, "because he looked tired." She went straight to him and kind of collapsed at his feet! Maybe she was trying to be as polite as she could. Maybe she was worn out from always having to be strong. Or maybe nothing had ever been as important to her as this. He hardly even looked at her.

She started to beg and plead with him to make me well again, to get rid of this thing that was tormenting me. He looked at her then and he could tell that she wasn't one of them. My mum says she thought he was probably fed up at having his privacy invaded. Still, what he said to her was not a nice thing to say.

He said, first of all he had to feed the children, and it wasn't right to take their food and give it to the dogs. My mum's explained to me that what he meant was that all his power should go to helping his own people. He didn't have any to spare for the likes of us dog-people.

My mum says that when she heard those words, they loosed an arsenal of different thoughts firing around her mind. She was furious with him for being so rude when he wasn't in his own country at all, but in hers; but mostly because I wasn't a dog: I was her child. So she was hurt as well. I think she'd thought here was someone who might be able to get past all that "us and them" stuff. But somewhere, even deeper down than that, she still had hope, still believed he could do it. I told you: she doesn't give up. easily.

Quick as a flash, she came back at him: "Sir," she said, "even the pet dogs under the table eat the children's leftovers." (I can just hear her — very polite, but not about to let him get away with anything.) But as soon as she heard herself saying it, she thought, "Oh no, I've blown it now! Women aren't supposed to talk to men like this."

But then she noticed that he didn't seem to be angry. Actually he was laughing a little, like he admired her for standing up for herself. And there was something else in his eyes, my mum says, as if he'd seen something about himself that he didn't know before, as if he'd seen himself as she saw him. Maybe it gave him a shock, or maybe he was just big enough to admit that she'd got the better of him. Whatever.

Anyway, when he spoke next, his voice was much more gentle. "I like your answer," he said. "Go home, and you'll find your daughter's better now."

My mum just looked at him for a minute, probably the only time in her life she had been speechless. Then she said, "Thank you. Thank you." She rushed out of the house and bolted all the way home.

And the amazing thing was, he was right. I don't know how it happened, but I suddenly found myself very, very tired, and I lay down on my bed and went to sleep. When I woke up, my mum was there looking at me. I smiled at her, and she smiled back and gave me a hug. And I've been fine ever since.

We don't talk about it very much — we're too busy just getting on with our lives. But sometimes my mum goes quiet, and I know she's thinking about him, wondering what's happened to him and hoping he's all right.

As for me, I still don't have a clue what was going on. I'm very glad the man happened to be there, and it definitely made me more interested in his religion, because there must be something in it. But mostly I'm glad I've got the mum I've got. I don't know why or how he made me better, but I do know that none of it would have happened without my mum, and I know why *she* did it. She did it because she loves me.

I chose this story for several reasons. To begin with, it has a strong female component. It's about a woman and a girl, and the woman is someone who comes over as a strong, loving, and resourceful person. The girl could well be the same age as my daughter (thirteen years old), and I have a lot of sympathy for the pressures and changes going on for girls at around that age. It's also a story about Jesus' encounter with people of another culture, historically looked down on by the Israelites, a very "us and them" story. It's easy to see the modern parallels.

I am interested, too, because the episode seems to show Jesus as a man of his time, brought up in a culture which held what we now call racist attitudes. He doesn't look very good in it initially. But what I like is that Jesus has the openness to look honestly at his behaviour, see the flaw in it, and go beyond it. He has the courage and the humility to change, and to do the loving thing. That to me is a more Godlike quality than some sort of unreal, inhuman perfection, and it gives me hope for change in my life and my society.

Food for all

John M Hull

Bible references
Genesis 47.13–26; Exodus 16.2–36

When Joseph was a prisoner in Egypt, the Pharaoh had a dream in which he saw seven fat cows come up out of the River Nile. The fat cows had no sooner started to eat the green grass than up out of the river came seven lean, thin cows. The thin cows ate up the fat cows and then the Pharaoh awoke. Joseph was brought out of the dungeon in order to tell the meaning of the Pharaoh's dreams. Joseph explained to the Pharaoh that in the land of Egypt there would be seven years of wonderful harvests when everyone would have plenty to eat. These would be followed by seven years of famine when the crops would fail and people would get hungry. So the government should get ready, and store the spare food up during the seven good years so that in the seven years of hunger there would be enough to eat.

The Pharaoh was so pleased with Joseph that he put him in charge of all the food supplies. Joseph became a sort of minister of agriculture, minister of transport, and head of the government building department all at once. Joseph built huge storehouses for the food. Every city and town had a storehouse, and Joseph appointed people to gather up the food from all the farms and store it. At first, Joseph kept a record of how much food he had gathered, but after a while there was so much food that he couldn't count it any longer.

Soon the seven good years were over and the seven hungry years began. The famine was bad even right up in the land of Palestine where Joseph's relatives lived. Joseph made sure that his old father, his brothers, and their wives and families were all safely settled in Egypt, where there was plenty of food because of the storehouses.

By this time, the ordinary people were starting to be very short of food. They had eaten all their own supplies, and there was hardly anything in the shops. All the food was in the storehouses, with soldiers guarding them. So the leaders of the people went to Joseph and asked, "Please let us have some of the government food."

Joseph replied, "Well, you can have it all right, but you'll have to pay for it. It all belongs to the Pharaoh, you see, and I can't let you have it for nothing."

So the people paid for their food. Every time they ran out of food, they went back to Joseph with the rest of their money and bought some more food. At last, they had no money left. Joseph gathered up all the money into huge treasure houses, and the money belonged to the Pharaoh. So now, the people had no money, and yet they were still hungry.

By now, Joseph had been a very important man for quite some time. He had forgotten the days when he himself was hungry in the prison. Now he rode around in a golden chariot, and everywhere soldiers went in front of him shouting, "Bow down! Bow down before the great Lord Joseph!" It seemed that Joseph was only interested in making lots of money for the Pharaoh. Perhaps he didn't care about the poor people any longer.

Still the famine went on, and the people ate up their last crumbs of food. They went to Joseph and said, "We haven't any money left now, so you'll have to just give us the food."

"You haven't any money, that's true," Joseph answered, "but you've got other things. What about your cows and your mules, your pigs and your chickens?"

So the people sold all their animals to Joseph in exchange for food. Lots of the animals had probably been killed already for food, but all the rest of the animals soon belonged to Joseph and Joseph gave them to the Pharaoh. For a while, the people had enough to eat. But still the famine went on, and still Joseph rode around in his golden chariot with the soldiers crying out, "Bow down!"

The next year, the people came to Joseph again. Now they had no food, no money, and no animals. What could they do? They offered Joseph their land. So Joseph bought all the land of the farmers and of the people who ran the little shops. In return, Joseph gave them food. So it was that the whole country of Egypt became the property of the Pharaoh. The Pharaoh now owned everything.

It's still rather like that in our world today. The rich people get richer and the poor get poorer. Huge piles of money are stored up in the rich countries of the world, while in the poor countries there is not enough to eat, and the rich people have bought even the land of the poor people, so everything they grow on the land now belongs to the rich. This is not a story any longer. These things are actually happening today in Africa, South America, and other parts of the world. Anyway, you want to hear the rest of the story about Joseph.

Finally, the people had nothing but their children and their own bodies. So they sold their children and themselves to the Pharaoh and became slaves. Many of the children died, just as many children in African countries are dying today. Years later, however, after Joseph had died, his descendants were mistreated in Egypt just as the people of Egypt had been. They themselves became slaves to the Pharaoh. But that is another story.

Once again, the people were hungry. The descendants of Joseph, hundreds of years later, had become slaves. They had escaped from Egypt into the desert, and there once again they felt the pangs of hunger. Indeed, they now looked back upon their slavery in Egypt, and it didn't seem quite so bad. At least they had something to eat there, even though they were slaves. Now they were free all right, but what was the point of being free if you were dying of hunger?

The people came to Moses, who was then their leader, and complained. This time they made their complaint to God as well. Moses did not behave as Joseph had behaved all those hundreds of years before. Moses did not say, "Give me your jewels and your necklaces and whatever money you've got left and I will see what I can do." Anyway, the people had no jewellery or money left. They had already given all their gold and silver to Aaron, Moses' brother and assistant, who had made a golden calf for the people to worship. So now, they had hardly anything left. Of course, Moses could have said that he would buy their children and their bodies and make them all slaves, but this was not Moses' idea. The people had been brought out of Egypt for freedom, not for more slavery.

So God said to Moses, "I have heard the cry of the people and I know how hungry they are. Tomorrow morning, I will rain bread down upon them from the clouds." In the morning, when the people came out of their tents, there was a heavy dew. As the dew melted, they saw that the ground was covered with a white, flaky substance. The people gathered it up and tasted it. It was a bit like the honey frosties that you have for breakfast. The people called the frosties "manna" because in their language that meant "What is it?"

Moses said, "This is the bread which God has given you. It will fall nearly every morning, and you must gather it up and eat it during the day. It will not last until the next day. Every day you must gather it up fresh."

So the people did as Moses said. The bread came down every morning. It did not matter whether a family was large or small, whether the family was thought to be an important family or whether it was a little, insignificant family. The bread fell for everyone.

Some people were greedy and gathered up more than they really needed. Sometimes, people were anxious not to waste any and didn't gather up enough. But in the evening, it didn't seem to make any difference. Those who had gathered a lot had none left over, and those who had only gathered a little bit found that they had enough. There was no charge for the bread. It was God's free bread, given to everybody, just because they needed it.

This story makes me think of the day when there won't be hungry children who go to school without breakfast and rich children who waste good food because they have too much. It makes me think of a day when people will have enough. The needs of everyone will be met. The bread will be shared by people. Everyone will live together in peace and friendship. Is this possible?

I have chosen these two stories because of the contrasting values of food and money which they represent. The first story is about the economy of the Pharaoh. It describes a world in which everything is sucked up from the poorer people into the accumulated wealth of the tiny minority. In many ways it is an uncomfortable story because it shows how Joseph, who was delivered by God out of his own destitution and slavery, quickly forgot where he had come from and – perhaps determined never to be enslaved again – turned his power and authority into an instrument for the oppression of others.

Stories like this one are told again and again in the Bible, in the history of the world, and they continue today. The Bible tells how God repeatedly has heard the cry of the exploited peoples of the world and responded. It records the pattern of action and counter-action, the successive waves of liberation and oppression. This is why the Bible speaks so sharply to us, and why at the same time its message arouses resentment and hostility from the rich and powerful. Children are well able to grasp such ideas and such realities. However, children seldom realize that the Bible tells this kind of story.

The waves of liberation and oppression have also left their mark upon how the Bible stories are told and how we interpret them. Because it is the story both of kings and rulers and of the poor, the Bible contains a mixture of accounts which represent both points of view. Today, when the Bible is read in the rich countries of the world, the point of view of the rich is emphasized. But when the poor and exploited people of the world read the Bible, they notice in it things which we in the wealthy one-seventh of the world hardly notice at all. This bias in perspective is reflected in children's story books, and so the essential democratic and liberating thrust of God's revelation in the Bible is obscured from both adults and children.

The second story describes the economy of God. This is an economy of justice and sharing, where the needs of all are met. It gives us a vision of society where money is restored to its proper use as a means of sharing between people, and is no longer accumulated to create distorted patterns of wealth and poverty. The economy of God is also called the Kingdom of God. It is described by Jesus in the Sermon on the Mount. It is a utopian dream which has never been realized. Nevertheless, this utopian dream still calls humanity forward. Sometimes the dream takes secular forms, sometimes religious. This is why the faith which came from the Bible always looks to the future in hope.

Encounter

Dumbstruck Zachariah

Author
Frank Topping

Bible reference
Luke 1.5–25

I knew, of course,
as the words fell from my mouth,
I knew I should never have spoken.
That's the trouble with priests,
we talk too much.
Too keen to score academic points,
to demonstrate the wit, the depth of knowledge,
to have the last, clever word.

I never dreamed I would be chosen
to offer the deepest longings of my people,
the fragrant prayers that rise
from the Altar of Incense,
from the Sanctuary of the Holy Place.
I never dreamed.

The chance is so remote.
Every male descendant of Aaron — a priest,
and every priest eligible.
Twenty-four family "courses" and in every "course"
Fathers, sons, grandfathers and great-grandfathers,
brothers, nephews, cousins by the dozen,
and one is chosen, at random, by lot.
Older men than me have closed their eyes
for the last time

and never heard their name called
for that most sacred duty.
I never dreamed
I would hear my name called out loud,
Zachariah En Kerem!

The guilt we carried, Elizabeth and I,
from some ancient, unknown sin.
Guilt made evident by our childless union
had, I believed, excluded me
from the holiest office a priest could hope for,
until I heard my name called, so clearly,
Zachariah En Kerem!

It was the greatest day in my life as a priest.
I passed, in a dream, through the Court of the Gentiles,
across the Women's Court,
unaware of hands, feet, or faces.
If men prayed in the Court of Israel, I did not hear them.
The eyes and ears of my mind saw only
the altar of the Court of Priests, whose fire,
carried to the sanctuary, would breathe life
into the incense of prayer.

I climbed the steps to the sanctuary,
and paused to compose myself.
I had waited all my life for this day,
I needed to remind myself
to savour every moment.

The Altar of Incense stands in the centre of the Sanctuary,
to the south of it, the seven lamps,
to the north, the table of shewbread.
It is a replica, in miniature, of the altar in the priest's court,
exact in every way, even to the horns of the altar.

At first, I did not see him.
He was standing to the right of the altar
but when I turned my head, the sight of him,
robbed me of breath,

contracted every muscle in my body.
I thought I would never breathe again.
Nothing in a lifetime of dreams,
neither ecstasy nor pain's extremes,
had prepared me for such a vision.

He spoke,
and it was the mellowest sound.
And yet restrained, as if that voice
could call upon mountains for power
and the sea for depth.
"Do not be afraid, Zachariah.
God has heard your prayer.
Elizabeth will bear you a son
and you will call him John.
Strong and mighty,
he will herald the coming of the Lord,
and prepare his way."

And I *questioned* him, even in my terror.
Questioned *him*!
"How can this be?" I said.
"I am old and Elizabeth is well stricken in years,
How can it be?"

And then that terrible voice spoke again:

"I am Gabriel," he said.
"I stand in the presence of God.
The words I speak are his words.
You, for your unbelief, shall not speak,
no word will cross your lips
till the word of God is accomplished."

And I could not, and did not — speak,
until the moment I heard the first cry
of our new-born child, our son, John,
whose voice, one day, would herald the coming
of the anointed one,
the Messiah.

That is my story, believe it as you will,
I am not concerned.
But, a word to the wise,
never, never argue — with an Archangel.

In recent years, I have attempted to view a number of events narrated in the New Testament through the eyes of the people involved in the stories. Sometimes characters on the fringe of a story open up a huge and fascinating area of research.

Perhaps it is the detective work that I enjoy most. To understand people, to appreciate why they said what they said or did what they did, demands some insight into their way of life, their culture, the religious and social pressures and demands they would face in the day-to-day business of surviving. It requires judging in what ways their family background, their history and tradition would inevitably influence their thinking, their decisions, their words, and actions.

For me, a great deal of excitement lies in breaking through the formal historical and factual accounts of events and entering into the thoughts, and listening to the everyday conversation, of the people involved, primarily because I am a storyteller rather than an historian, though the two disciplines overlap somewhat.

There is an argument which suggests that all history is at the mercy of politicians, of one kind or another, in that what is recorded for posterity is likely to be what the political power of the day wants to be recorded, and if you want to know what was really going on in any particular period, you would be far better off reading historical fiction rather than politically doctored "fact", because it is the storyteller who captures feelings, hopes and dreams, and in so doing takes us into the very heart of history.

My hope would be to become so familiar with how people spent their days that, if there were a time-slip and one came face to face with a character one was studying, it might actually be possible to enter into a reasonably sensible conversation with them.

The culture and life-style of Zachariah, and what little of his history is referred to in the New Testament is full of possibilities for the historical storyteller. Zachariah is a priest. (A huge area to explore: where does he work? what does he do? is there a hierarchy? what would his "job prospects" have amounted to?) He and Elizabeth are an elderly, childless couple. (How would this be interpreted by the society in which they lived?) Given that Zachariah is a priest, the fact that an angel is part of the story is perhaps not so surprising, but what is an angel? And what would Zachariah have believed about visions?

The worldly wise and cynical would question and doubt those who talk of visions and dreams, but what are visions other than images and thoughts passing before the mind's eye? How else can we assess situations except through the mind and with imagination? If God does not speak through the imagination, how else is he to be heard? In George Bernard Shaw's play, *St Joan*, Joan of Arc is asked to confess that her "voices" are entirely in her imagination, and Joan replies, "Of course they are. How else would I hear them?"

Elijah on the mountain of the Lord

Terence Copley

Bible reference
1 Kings 19.1–13

Elijah was running scared. He had good reason to be. The all-powerful Queen Jezebel had put out a contract on his life the minute she heard from her husband, the all-weakly King Ahab, that Elijah had been involved in the events that had led to a mob of sightseers killing four hundred and fifty prophets of Baal – Jezebel's god, Jezebel's prophets.

The words of her message echoed in Elijah's ears as he ran: "So may the gods do to me – and more as well – if I don't make your life like those dead prophets by this time tomorrow."

"By this time tomorrow . . . By this time tomorrow . . ." The words went through his mind like his mother's sharp knife used to cut through goat's milk cheese when he was a boy, like the sharp knives that cut the throats of those prophets of Baal.

So now he was on the run. Elijah: the once-victorious prophet, spokesperson for the Holy One, the God whose name was too sacred to say aloud, the different God, who seemed to have ended months of drought, seemed to have set fire to a sacrificed bull, seemed to have proved his existence and power so completely that even the spectators were convinced by what they saw with their own eyes.

Where was this God now? If Elijah hadn't used his legs and run, he would already be dead. It was he who decided to run, past the border town of Beer-sheba and into the Negev Desert, beyond the reach of Jezebel and her agents. No God had given him that idea. No God had rescued him. Even his own name, Elijah, meaning "My God is the Lord", seemed to mock him now. What sort of Lord lets you down like this? He felt completely alone. But he could not leave Jezebel's words behind: "So may the gods do to me – and more as well – if I don't make your life like those dead prophets by this time tomorrow."

There would be people searching for him, perhaps a reward for his capture, dead or alive. If he asked nomads for food, even here in the desert, word would spread: a stranger, not of their tribe, would stand out. There'd be difficult questions: What are you doing here? Where are you from? Who *are* you?

It was a chilling thought: you're never alone, even in a desert. Yet if he didn't ask for food, he'd die anyway. How long can a person survive in desert conditions? Sooner or later he'd be driven back, back to Jezebel's country and into her power.

Lost in his thoughts, Elijah sat down under the shade of a solitary broom tree. He felt weary in body and spirit. He started to pray, not the confident prayer of the defeater of the prophets of Baal, but the prayer of a defeated runaway: "I've had enough. Now, Lord, take away my life. I'm no better than any of my ancestors."

He lay down under the shade of the tree and fell into the deep sleep of exhaustion. He didn't know how long he had slept, but suddenly he felt – or did he dream? – someone shaking him, saying "Get up! Eat!"

He roused himself. There by his head was a cake of bread baked on hot stones, and a jar of water. He ate and drank speedily, greedily, needily. Then, still tired, he lay down again. Another deep, apparently dreamless, sleep. But he was being shaken awake – or dreaming? – again.

"Get up! Eat! Or else the journey will be too much for you!" Journey? What journey? He got up. Ate again. Drank again. Then set off.

Day merged into dusk, dusk into night, night into dawn, dawn to noon-time heat, then dusk, night, dawn, noon time. On and on. Dawn, noon, dusk, night. Dawn, noon, dusk, night. On and on.

It was said in the after-time that Elijah travelled forty days and forty nights in the strength of that food and water until he reached Horeb, the Mountain of the Lord. When he arrived, it was night. He noticed what looked like a cave entrance or cleft in the rock – it was hard in the dark to be sure which – though it offered shelter. This Mountain of the Lord was an eerie place, but at least no one could get at him there. He dozed uneasily, passing the night there.

In the morning, still in his rock refuge, just as he was comforting himself that he was alone on this great mountain and wondering about eating, he heard a voice. Close to him. As close as conversation. It was totally unnerving.

It spoke to him by name. "What are you doing here, Elijah?"

Who else was on the mountain? Who knew his name? Who knew he was here? Had he been followed? Where could he run now? Solid rock behind him, the voice coming from his only exit. The question haunted him: "What are you doing here, Elijah?" What *was* he doing there? Elijah had to answer. Deep down inside, he knew where the voice came from.

"I've been – " His voice was tense, higher than he intended, so he started again. "I've been trying to defend the Lord with all my energy." He swallowed nervously and continued bitterly, "The Israelites have broken their solemn agreement with you (did he realize he'd slipped into the word 'you'?), destroyed your altars, and killed your spokespeople with the sword. I'm the only one left. There's nobody else. Even now they're searching for me, to kill me."

If he thought he was making a "You've got to help me" speech, it didn't work. The speaker seemed to ignore his answer completely and carried on with the message "Go out and stand on the mountain in front of the Lord, for the Lord is about to pass by."

Elijah didn't answer. With the protection of solid rock, he felt sheltered from the power and force of God's glory. Even the great Moses, who came to this mountain long ago, had been shielded from God's glory. Now he, Elijah, the runaway let-God-down, was under orders to stand outside in the open. To stand in the presence of the Living God? Elijah would have found a return to Jezebel's territory less frightening. Against a person you might stand a chance, but who could look at God and live?

Elijah found his thoughts were being invaded, at first by a whisper, then a swoosh, a woosh – suddenly there was a storm-force wind, so strong that rocks were broken in pieces, entire mountain sides collapsed, boulders rolled, dust whirled round till he could hardly see. Elijah felt himself being tugged off his feet into this gravity-defying gale. But the Lord was not present in the wind and after a time it died down.

Hardly had Elijah got his balance and breath back than he felt a slight tremor under his feet. The ground was starting to move. Very quickly it was rocking, thumping, pounding, bumping! Here a chasm, there a crater – how could he remain standing in the earthquake? But the Lord was not in the earthquake either. Before Elijah could stop quaking himself – from fear and from the movement of the ground – a crackling, smoke-swirling fire spluttered, then roared, through the dry grasses and parched bushes of the desert mountain. Black smoke and flames filled the hillsides. The sky was hidden. The roaring flames were consuming everything in their path. It seemed to the coughing, choking Elijah that fire was everywhere. But the Lord was not in the fire. Hurricane, earthquake, fire, and in all of them noise.

After all that, the most terrifying thing of all:

> A sound
> of sheer
> silence

When Elijah heard it, he wrapped his face in his cloak and walked right out of his refuge in the rock. It was as if the silence was shouting. He knew that at last, like it or not, he might hear the voice of the Lord God himself . . .

As a member of the Religious Society of Friends (Quakers), I belong to a religious tradition that worships on the basis of silence. Our meetings for worship are largely silent, sometimes entirely so. Quaker experience is that when mind and body are stilled, the voice of God can be heard by any truly listening person, old or young, female or male, Quaker or non-Quaker. Sometimes the voice can be heard with absolute clearness; sometimes not. But God doesn't live in silence any more or less than in noise. Silence just creates conditions whereby we can hear God better, as it did for Elijah. The message Elijah received, like the message we may receive, is not always the one we want to hear. God is not an echo of our own wishes but, to use human language, "has a mind of his own"! The question is, are we listening?

The parable of the prodigal father

Maurice Lynch

Bible reference
Luke 15.11–32

There was this man and he had two sons. The youngest seldom got things right. Everything he touched seemed to go wrong for him. Indeed, his name and his mistakes were constantly on the lips of all in the village. The eldest was as secret as soil. He must have made mistakes, too, but if he did, no one ever heard of them. And the father – the father loved them both. It was late one evening when the boys came to him: "You're not getting any younger," they told him. "We want no rows when you're gone. You could split the farm between us now." And he did.

A few days later, the young fellow came home, late. Awkwardly, he stood in front of his father and announced that he was leaving in the morning. The father pulled himself slowly from the chair, threw both arms round the boy's neck and poured himself out, crying. The boy stood stiff, unyielding, thinking there was no need for such a scene. The eldest watched from the corner and thought: "If it was me that was going, the old man would not shed a tear."

In the morning, the young fellow took off for the far country. Now he was no Jacob. Jacob could take a lamb or goat and mastermind them into a herd, but this young man just let the whole inheritance flow through his fingers like water. When the famine came, there was no Pharaoh to give him a post minding granaries. He was lucky to find a job minding pigs. And he'd have eaten the slop they gave the pigs but the farmer watched and would not let him. Then, in his hunger, he thought of home and the grain in all his father's barns. "I will go to my father," he said. "I will tell him I've wronged him. Take me back as a hired servant. I am not worthy to be known as your son." With the words etched on his mind, he took the road for home.

On the hill, beside the house, the father sat. He had sat there often before, eyes always strained on the corner of the road. When the boy turned it, the father knew his step from a thousand others. Tunic hitched around his knees, he raced to him. Again, the hands were on the boy's shoulders and the father weeping.

"Father, I have sinned against heaven and you. I am no longer worthy to be called your son," the boy pleaded.

"Bring him out a new robe," the father called to the servants. "And sandals for his feet, a ring for his finger, and we will kill the calf and call in all the neighbours. Today, my child that was dead has come to life again. For years he was lost and today we found him." In that house, that night, the feast just had to begin.

Now all this time, the eldest boy was in the fields, working. As dusk fell, he too came to the top of the hill, saw the lights in every window of the house, heard the music, smelt the food. He was sure his father had gone mad, but the servants told him of the brother's return. "Go, tell my father, I'll have no part in it," he commanded, bitterly.

Within minutes the father was at the door, tunic hitched again, running up the hill. The roar from the top almost drove him back to the bottom.

"All these years, all these years I've slaved for you. But not once, not once, in all that time did it cross your mind to find me a kid to celebrate with my friends. And then, that no-good comes home and you kill the calf and call in the neighbours. And I bet you think I'll join you. Well never, not ever."

Slowly, the father came to the boy, hands now on both his shoulders. Earnestly, he pleaded. "Lad, you are always with me and everything I have is yours. But if a brother dies and comes to life again, if a son is lost and then found, can't you see: we have to celebrate?" But there was no give on this son's face.

Suddenly, the father felt tired. He turned slowly, to walk down the hill. As he did, the door opened and out came the youngest son. The tunic had fallen from the shoulder, the ring barely clung to the famine-thin finger. But what the father noticed most was the lost look on his face. He was home but no longer recognized the place. The father looked from the lost face of one child to that of the other, the slave on the top of the hill. Then, suddenly, for the first time that evening, he became aware of the music from the feast that none of them was at, drifting in the air.

The music went to his heart and from his heart to his feet and there on the hill the old man began to dance. As he danced, he prayed that the joy in his heart at the presence again of both his children, might find their hearts too, and bring them home truly to him for they were his very all.

The parable of the prodigal father seems to me one of the most central stories of Christianity. It conveys simply, yet profoundly, the Christian vision of God. I have always felt that an emphasis on forgiveness as its central theme was misplaced. A love that is unconditional, and yet so difficult to accept and believe in, seems to match better the depths of this story. At another level, it accurately reflects human experience. Few who hear it can fail to identify their own place in the story. There is sympathy for that eldest boy, steady, reliable, anxious for the needs of a father whose constant concern seems to be the fate of his youngest son. When the father heaps rewards on the returning runaway, one senses and approves the anger of that brother at the unfairness of it all. Then, which of us does not know the younger boy? He always was the pet, who knew just the right tone of voice, and words and looks to get his way with the father. Then there is the father who loves them both, but neither really believes him. For the eldest boy believes that love has to be earned, the youngest that it requires guile and flattery. Neither sees that it is a gift offered without conditions. There is no catch or trap. It is to that vision that the father calls each, because only then will he be truly a father for them, only then, they truly sons to him.

Over the lake

Christopher Herbert

Bible references
Matthew 14.13–33 (Mark 6.30–52; Luke 9.10–17; John 6.1–21)

One day, when Jesus was with his disciples by the Lake of Galilee, a messenger came to tell him that John the Baptist had been killed by Herod. Jesus was deeply troubled by the news and decided that he wanted to be on his own so that he could pray and think about John. He asked his disciples to get a boat ready and to take him across to the other side of the lake.

In the boat he was very quiet and sat with his head bowed; the disciples too were silent. They could hear the wind rippling the sails and the water splashing against the prow of the boat. No one spoke, everyone was deep in thought.

But as they drew close to the shore they could see that, instead of Jesus finding a place to be on his own, there were crowds and crowds of people waiting for him. Jesus sighed very deeply. He so much wanted to be alone but he could not avoid the people's demands.

As he stepped out of the boat, the disciples tried to make a way for him through the crowds. But Jesus stopped them and first one person and then another came to kneel at his feet for him to lay his hands on them. The disciples watched Jesus carefully: they saw him pray with each person, they saw the lines of distress and tiredness on his face, but they saw that everyone who came to him was blessed.

It was late in the afternoon and the sun began to set, firing the hills with golden light. And still the crowds would not let Jesus alone. He ached with tiredness and love for these people. The disciples tried to protect him: "Master," they said, "It's getting very late now. Please send the people away before it gets too dark – and tell them to buy themselves some supper."

"What?" said Jesus. "Tell these people to go away? How can I? There's no need for them to go away; *you* give them something to eat."

The disciples were puzzled by what he said. They looked at each other: none of them had brought much food and certainly not enough for such a crowd.

"Look," said Peter, laughing, "all we've got between us is five loaves and two fish. . ." The others laughed as well because they, too, were getting hungry and didn't want to give away their meagre picnic.

"Bring the loaves and fishes to me," said Jesus. Peter took the five loaves and two fish in a small woven basket and handed it to Jesus. And then Jesus told the crowds to sit down. The disciples stood around, wondering what was going to happen next.

Jesus waited until everyone was absolutely silent and looking at him. Then he took the loaves and the fishes, blessed them, broke them in pieces and gave the pieces to the disciples. "Take these," he said, "and give them to the people."

The disciples went from person to person handing out pieces of bread and fish; everyone ate and everyone was satisfied. The people laughed, talked, and grew noisy but, as sometimes happens in crowds, there came a time when they all grew quiet and still, wondering what had really happened. And all the while Jesus looked at the people with eyes filled with compassion. He thought of John – and of that moment when he, Jesus, had been baptized by him. He remembered that in the desert John had feasted on locusts and wild honey. What would John have said if he could have seen Jesus feeding all these people with a new kind of manna? John's life may have ended in a brutal murder, but Jesus was ready to follow John's work and feed everyone who came to him in need.

The disciples came to Jesus, amazed at the crowd, amazed at the feast, and even more amazed at all the things that were whirling around in their minds — all those questions: Was Jesus a new Moses? Was Jesus a king? Was Jesus the Messiah? But they didn't dare to ask him. Instead, they waited.

"Once you've cleared up," he said, "it will be time to go. . ." The crowds began to disperse — a group here, a group there — standing up, waving to Jesus before in the gathering darkness they made their way home. But before everyone had gone, Jesus said to the disciples, "It's time for you to go as well. I need to stay here on my own."

He turned his back to the lake and walked slowly up into the hills and sank to his knees in exhaustion. His tiredness became his prayer as, thinking about John's death, he prayed that God's will would be done. For a long while he stayed amongst the rocks, looking up into the starlit heavens, praying to God his Father.

And then slowly, very slowly, he made his way back to the lake shore.

The disciples, meanwhile, were some way from the land, rowing back across the lake but making little headway against a very strong wind that had blown up. Clouds scudded across the sky and the waves were whipped into a fury by the wind. Some of the disciples were afraid and suggested that Peter ought to have known better than to have set out on such a dangerous night.

"Thought you said we'd be all right," yelled one of them to Peter.

"I've never known a night like it," cried Peter, the spray lashing against his face.

And then they saw Jesus walking on the sea towards them. They were terrified. "It's a ghost!" they screamed, as the wind moaned in the rigging and the waves tossed the boat in a frenzy.

But Jesus spoke to them through the turmoil: "Don't be afraid," he said, "it is me," and he stepped into their boat and joined them.

At that very moment the wind ceased, the waves grew still, and everything was at peace. The disciples were astonished and gazed on Jesus with love and with awe.

I chose the stories of the feeding of the five thousand and the walking on the water because they are so awe-inspiring and so puzzling. No matter which way we approach the stories, they retain their ability to reveal Jesus' authority and power. And yet both stories are set in the context of a time of great personal sadness for Jesus. John the Baptist had been a major figure in Jesus' life. Now, after John's murder by Herod, Jesus must have felt he also was very vulnerable. In his grief and perplexity, all he would have wanted to do was to be on his own with his close friends; no pressures, no expectations. But it was not to be. Instead, he was confronted by crowds, hungry for healing and longing for his touch. His heart went out to them – and he took all the supplies there were (and they were meagre enough) and after prayer the people were "satisfied".

You can read this story in a number of ways: as a nature miracle; as no more than a story of the Kingdom party to be held in heaven; as a foretaste (note the word) of the eucharist; or as an acted parable about sharing. The story demands serious exploration. And then, having satisfied the people, Jesus at last has time to be entirely on his own.

There then follows the equally perplexing story of the walking on the water. Again it can be approached in a number of ways: as a nature miracle; as a legend having no basis in historical fact; or as an allegory of the way in which Jesus brings peace when we are most in turmoil.

Simply as stories, then, these are gems; and I believe they can be used with children for their story quality alone. But they can and should be explored, not just as texts, but as stories layered with meaning. They are essentially theological: they exist to tell us something about Jesus and about how his earliest followers regarded him, but they also have the capacity to challenge us today and to ask what kind of a person he must have been to have such stories told about him.

Jonah goes deeper

Douglas Charing

Bible reference
Jonah 1.1–4.11

Jonah was a prophet in Israel who told his people about their God. One day, God called to him: "Jonah, go to Nineveh. The people there are unkind to each other and have done wicked things. Tell them God says to behave better or they will be punished."

But Jonah did not want to go. Instead, he went down to the harbour and decided to get on a ship going in the opposite direction from Nineveh. His ship was going to Tarshish. God would not find him there! So Jonah found a bed on board the ship and went to sleep.

The ship set sail. Suddenly the wind began to blow and, before long, the ship was caught in the middle of a mighty storm. The sailors became very worried, yet Jonah slept on. The storm became so strong that the ship began to break apart. And still Jonah slept on. The sailors were now very frightened and began to pray to their gods. And still Jonah slept on. At last, with the boom of the waves and the shuddering of the ship, Jonah awoke and realized all this was his fault.

"Throw me into the sea and the storm will go away," said Jonah to the captain.

But the captain refused: "You will drown, no one can swim in such an angry sea."

The storm was getting even worse. Again Jonah advised the captain to throw him overboard: "You will reach dry land safely if you throw me overboard," he insisted.

"Very well," said the captain, "but I do it with a heavy heart."

Once Jonah was gone, the waves grew smaller, the thunder stopped, and the lightning did not flash any more. In a short time, the sun came out and the sea was peaceful. The ship's crew were now able to continue their journey and got safely to port.

Jonah was now in the water, but God caused a big fish to swallow him up. Behind him Jonah heard water wooshing out through the fish's gills, as Jonah carried on travelling down the muscly tunnel to the fish's stomach.

Jonah found the inside of the fish very comfortable. He could look out through its eyes and see other fish and plants, and even shipwrecks lying on the sea bottom. The belly of the fish was warm and well-lit by layers of sparkling diamonds that it had swallowed.

For three days, the fish took Jonah on a sightseeing trip through the oceans of the world. Jonah was so busy looking around that he forgot God was angry with him and that he was being punished. Suddenly, a giant fish, larger than Jonah's, came racing after them. She was a mother fish, carrying a load of 365,000 little ones. God had sent her to take Jonah away from the first friendly fish.

Against his will, Jonah had to move to the belly of the bigger fish. In the twinkling of an eye, he was coughed from his comfortable surroundings and shot through the water into the open mouth of the mother fish. Here his new home smelt very fishy and was rather crowded, with so many baby fish. He soon remembered God and said: "All right, God, I give up. I will go to Nineveh. Just get me out of this fish!"

God heard Jonah's thoughts and caused the fish to spew Jonah up on to the beach. Once again God told Jonah to go to Nineveh, and this time Jonah went.

The people of Nineveh heard Jonah's message, and decided to stop their evil ways. They began to love each other; they began to help each other; they said sorry for all the hurt they had done to others. They had truly repented and this pleased God who decided not to punish them.

Was Jonah pleased? Not at all. In fact, he was very angry: "These people are not worth saving," he muttered to himself. "God had no right to forgive them. They should have been punished."

But God felt that Jonah should be willing to give even bad people a second chance. "After all," said God, "I'm willing to do that; why shouldn't he?"

So God created a large gourd plant, and in the heat of the day, Jonah sat under it enjoying the shade it gave. In the morning, however, Jonah was in for a shock. The gourd lay on the ground all dried up. God had sent a worm that nibbled every last leaf until the tree was bare.

By now the sun was very hot and poor Jonah was hot and very angry. "God," he cried, "how could you let the gourd die? It gave me shade; its leaves kept me cool. Now it is gone and I am baking hot."

God replied in a stern voice: "The gourd grew up in a day; it died in a day. You are angry and sad that I killed a plant which gave you shade, but you, Jonah, are willing to let a whole city of people be destroyed. To me, Nineveh is more than a plant: it is a great city. Many people built it. Thousands live in it. They are all my children whom I love. It is true that the people of Nineveh did great wrongs, but they changed their ways and have returned to me. That's why I am willing to give the people there a chance to try again. Because of my love for them, I will now forgive them and not destroy them."

Jonah now understood the ways of God. "I did wrong too," he said, "I loved only the people of Israel. I now see that you, oh God, are the God of all peoples. I loved a plant more than I loved people. Forgive me, oh Lord." So Jonah was now also able to take pity on the people of Nineveh and forgive them. And for the first time this prophet of Israel realized that the God of the universe has compassion over all his creatures.

Perhaps it is because many people see the Book of Jonah as a whale of a tale, or even as a tale of a whale, that they treat it as something for children rather than for adults. Certainly it is a very entertaining story, one which is enjoyed by children. (The idea which I have borrowed from rabbinic stories, of there being two fish – one hospitable and one chock-full and smelly – adds to the amusement.) But its true message is very much for all ages.

A Jewish prophet is sent by what some may regard as the Jewish God to a Gentile city, to get them to repent and for God to forgive them. Jonah is the real sinner in that his concern is only for the Jewish people and not for the rest of humanity. In an eloquent and moral way, however, Jonah is made to understand that God is a universal God, and if any person repents of his sin, God will forgive. Jonah finally realizes that God is concerned not only for the Jews but also for "heathens" many miles from the land of Israel. The message of the book is of the love of a universal God for all peoples, and is therefore prophetic doctrine at its peak.

It is no accident that the Book of Jonah was chosen by the early rabbis to be the *haftara* (second reading) on Judaism's most sacred day, Yom Kippur. On that day, Jews know that true repentance can avert punishment if people sincerely change their behaviour.

The thankful gatecrasher

Elaine Storkey

Bible reference
Luke 7.36–50

The scene opens with a party. It is a quiet sort of party; people are relaxing around a table and eating and drinking.

The man who is giving the dinner, Simon the Pharisee, has invited Jesus as his guest, so we find him with the others sitting back and enjoying the food. In those days these dinners were quite public events. They would not be shut off in a room in someone's house, but usually held out of doors, in a courtyard. It was always warm, and much of the time people were outside. That meant other people nearby would see what was going on, and sometimes, if there was a special guest, there might be quite a crowd gathering to see the celebrity.

On this particular day, the word had got around that Jesus was the guest and one woman especially wanted to be there to see him. It was quite a risky thing to do, because she was a "person with a past". In fact, her reputation had not been very good. A lot of religious people looked down on her. Still, she was determined. She wanted to see Jesus. She didn't come empty-handed, either: she brought with her a very valuable jar which contained expensive perfume.

She must have stood with others in the crowd for a few minutes and watched the people at the dinner. Then suddenly, without warning, she went forward as if she was going to join the party. But she stopped behind Jesus and knelt down on the ground, crying and weeping. Before anyone knew what was happening, she had started to touch Jesus's feet, bending her head over them, letting her tears drop and gently stroke them.

Then, she opened the perfume and the whole company of people could smell its powerful aroma. You can imagine how horrified they were at what followed. She let down her beautiful, long hair, with it she wiped his feet and kissed them and then poured the perfume all over them, massaging and touching his skin.

At this point, Simon, the man who had invited Jesus, had seen enough. He felt outraged. This woman was behaving like a prostitute at his dinner, lavishing perfume and kissing this man's feet. It was a public disgrace and Jesus was not even asking her to go away. He thought to himself, "This is no prophet! No respectable man, let alone a man of God, would ever allow this sort of contact from a woman like her."

No sooner had he had these thoughts, than Jesus spoke to him. He wanted to ask him a question. The question concerned an imaginary moneylender who had two clients. One of these clients owed the moneylender about ten thousand pounds, the other owed him one thousand. But they were both absolutely broke and couldn't repay him, so the moneylender let them both off.

"Now," asked Jesus, "Which one of these two would love him more?"

It was an easy question and Simon well knew the answer. But he was cautious in his reply: "I *suppose*," he said, "the one who had been let off the bigger amount." He wasn't quite sure what was coming.

"Yes, quite right," said Jesus, and then he got Simon to look at the woman. Now he had some strong words he wanted to say to him.

"I came to your house," he said, "and wasn't treated with very warm hospitality. Even though my feet were dry and dusty from the road, you didn't give me any water to wash them." (Simon must have winced. Everybody got a bowl of water when they arrived at a dinner. It was common courtesy.)

"Anyway," Jesus continued, "this woman made up for you because she washed my feet with her tears and she wiped them dry with her hair.

"What's more, you didn't greet me with a kiss." (Another wince from Simon. It was customary to embrace your guests warmly when they arrived: rather like shaking hands, or smiling and saying welcome.)

"And again," said Jesus, "this woman made up for you. Because from the time I entered she hasn't stopped kissing my feet. And finally, you didn't put oil on my head." (This was the final blow to Simon's pride. Rubbing oil on to tired skin was regarded as generous and relaxing. Jesus had noticed all his lapses in hospitality.)

"But," Jesus continued, "she poured perfume even on my feet."

He stopped here. There was more to what he was saying than just telling Simon off for not being very welcoming. Jesus wanted to get to his story about the moneylender. So out came the main point.

"Here is a person whose many sins have been forgiven. You can tell that, because look how much she loves. Other people, who haven't been forgiven much, don't love much." And turning to the woman he repeated to her: "Your sins are forgiven."

The point, of course, was not lost on Simon. Here was a man who lived by the law: a religious leader, a Pharisee, an upright man, but also a bit self-righteous. Very often self-righteous people are not good at being forgiven because they are not good at admitting they are wrong. But this woman with a bad past had no problem in recognizing *she* needed forgiveness nor in calling to God to help her. And the result was she loved Jesus: she saw in him someone very special, very holy, and someone who loved other people. She felt accepted and forgiven by him. He brought her back to God.

The other guests, sadly, were too stuck in their outrage about what had happened to get the point of Jesus' words. Instead of recognizing that they needed forgiveness too, they just muttered to each other and complained about Jesus, "Who does he think he is: going about forgiving people's sins?" But Jesus' attention was on the woman who had poured out all her love on him. With gentleness and understanding he affirmed all she had done for him and showed how much he admired and respected her. For he said, "It is your faith that has saved you." Then, making sure that nothing that anyone else had said would upset or disturb her, he gave her the blessing and love she longed for:

"Go in peace."

I have chosen this story because I think it gives us an unexpected glimpse of what God is like. It shows that the way God values people is very different from the way they can be valued by the society around them. When I first came across it many years ago I was struck by the interesting relationship between the three main characters – Jesus, a woman who isn't given a name, and a religious leader called Simon – and by the difference between Jesus and all the other men in the story. Jesus sees things that everyone else misses. I have always appreciated this, for it shows us that God cares less about what is on the surface of people's lives than about what they are like inside. It also says something very special about the way God values women, even when others around them do not.

Destiny

Huldah's warning

Catherine Bowness

Bible references
2 Kings 22.1–23.33 (2 Chronicles 34.1–36.3)

I have a special gift. Sometimes I wish I could give it away, to someone else, but that would be impossible. I also think it would be a cruel thing to do. You see, this gift does not bring me joy. God allows me to know the future.

It is an awesome burden. When I see terrible crimes committed throughout my homeland and hear many people utter wicked things against the Lord, I know what will happen to them but I am unable to speak. Sometimes it is difficult being a woman of God. Only when the time is right is a prophetess allowed to tell the plans of the Lord. She may only watch and wait. How can I express the pain this brings?

Once, many years ago, I knew my knowledge could save the nation from itself. I wanted to shout it from the rooftops. I would have climbed the highest mountain to proclaim the word of God! All I needed was a sign. I was not given one. I was simply told to remain silent until Josiah's team of officials came to my house seeking wisdom.

My husband's family had royal connections. Grandfather had been the Keeper of the Wardrobe, a worthy position within the royal household. That is how I knew about the goings on at court – how each new king led the people further away from God. Then Josiah came to the throne.

A nasty business it was too, Josiah's succession. He was eight years old, an innocent child. His father, a wicked and unpopular man, even by today's standards, had been assassinated by his own courtiers. Judah was a corrupt place in those days, but from the moment he sat on the throne, Josiah began to follow the ways of his great ancestor, David. He wanted to do the will of God. Yes, a good king he was, young Josiah. He did his best for

Judah, though even he could not save our beloved land from the fate I had foreseen.

Josiah spent his whole reign trying to lead his people back to God. When he was twenty-six and had been king for eighteen years, he decided to renovate the Temple. He didn't use slave labour either, but arranged for all the workforce to be paid fairly in melted down Temple silver. Many carpenters, builders, and stonemasons took part in the project. The Temple was to be made fit to be the house of God. I watched and outwardly rejoiced, though in my heart the knowledge I carried weighed heavily upon me.

During the renovations a scroll was discovered. It must have lain forgotten in the Temple for many a year. Hilkiah, the High Priest, examined it with care. Then he began to recognize the words. In his hand he held the old book of the Law! It was the find of a lifetime. It contained all the rules for living according to the will of God. In great excitement he sought out Shaphan, the King's adjutant-general, and gave it to him.

"You must read this!" he insisted.

And read it Shaphan did, aloud to King Josiah himself. It wasn't a comfortable read, either. There, in ancient handwriting, were all the rules which the people of Judah had forgotten. The rules which they were breaking every day! The rules that even members of the royal household had neglected. There were even rules that no one had heard before. This whole way of life had been thrown away!

You should have seen the expressions on the faces in the throne room! Men and women looked at their feet and waited in silence for the king to speak.

But the king . . . said . . . nothing.

He rose from the throne and tore his clothes in shame, horror, and despair. If so much sin and wickedness existed, how could he lead the people back to God?

At last he said, "God will be so angry. Our grandparents and parents have broken all the laws."

Then he sent his officials to me, Huldah of Jerusalem, the prophetess. Finally, God told me that it was time to speak and my burden was lifted. How the words fell from my lips:

"God is going to bring disaster to the land," I cried. "The people turned away from him and offered sacrifices to other gods. The Lord is very angry!"

The king's men looked at me in horror. Poor, helpless creatures, perhaps they hoped for mercy. For the king himself I had some words of comfort. However, they were not my own words. When I opened my mouth, out poured the voice of God.

"Tell the king of Judah: because you wept and tore your clothes before me I have listened to you. This is the word of the Lord. You will die in peace and will not live to see the terrible things that will happen."

It was all rather dramatic. There was a slight pause, the officials looked at me and then at each other. Then, without another word, they rushed back to court to tell the king. The king ordered a huge public meeting. Every person living in Jerusalem had to be there. It took place in the Temple. There the king himself read aloud the scroll of the Law. The people listened. This was serious! The scroll left the listeners in no doubt. They were in big trouble! Those who had broken the laws of Moses would be punished. Many were ashamed at the behaviour of the nation.

The king made a solemn promise to God that day. He said that every law on the scroll would be kept from now on. All the people made the same promise and Josiah began a clean-up campaign. I expect you know the sort of thing I mean. He encouraged new moral standards, setting a good example himself, of course. The nation pulled together and worked harder. All the fancy statues, set up in honour of the sun, the moon, and a great miasma of other gods, were pulled down. Wicked priests, especially those rumoured to have carried out human sacrifices, were hunted down. Prostitutes, both female and male, were turned out of their homes. So-called sacred stones were ground into dust. No effort was spared in the quest to destroy wickedness.

That year we had such a Passover festival I'm certain the country had not seen the like since the time of Moses himself. We wore the correct clothes. All the special food was served. Every word on the scroll of the Law was obeyed. It was a time of renewal. The good old days were remembered. We had a new beginning!

We went from strength to strength. My heart lifted as I saw and heard about the deeds of Josiah. The nation had turned to God. Disaster had been averted.

Or so the people thought. In reality, it had only been postponed.

Now can you see why I told you that the gift of prophecy is not an easy thing with which to live? Remember, even in the midst of all the rejoicing, I knew too many things – that these times wouldn't last, that this king would die, and the people would forget their fine promises. I knew his son would sin and the nation would follow. Ordinary people look to the example set by their political leaders. One does not have to be a prophetess to work that out: that's simple common sense.

No king has ever worked as hard as young Josiah to keep the Law given to us by Moses. Thirty-nine he was when Pharaoh Neco killed him at Megiddo. They brought his body back to Jerusalem in a chariot. The streets flowed with our tears.

I, Huldah, prophetess of God, knew what would follow. How my heart ached!

Three short months his son reigned and in three months the kingdom returned to wickedness.

Here is a story of contrasts. There is great joy when the scroll of the Law is found, but sadness and shame when its contents are read. A strong leader encourages the people to behave well and work together but a weak one allows them to slip back into wickedness, while the person with religious insight watches the events with sadness. God has given human beings free will and sometimes they use it with cataclysmic consequences.

I think this is one of the most tragic stories in the Bible because the writer has captured a deep flaw in human nature. People often look back to the "old days" and aim to follow the example set by previous generations. Parents and grandparents may have made mistakes, but this new generation will revive the values of much earlier times! Often political leaders make stirring speeches encouraging us to remember the spirit of the past. The media take up the call, society takes a long hard look at itself and appears to make an effort to set high moral standards. Being good becomes fashionable! It does not last. Someone exposes a weakness in the leader or perhaps some people become bored with goodness. It is no longer newsworthy! Society returns to its usual ways until a new leader makes a stirring speech and puts it to shame.

I find this a good story to share with young people. I ask them if Josiah's people would have continued to behave well had their king lived into old age. "It depends," they reply and a fierce debate follows on what makes us good, bad, or "sort of in the middle"!

In the beginning

Anthony Phillips

Bible reference
Genesis 1.1–2.4a

Before time began, there was nothing. The earth was a watery wasteland in utter darkness without any form of life. Then the spirit of God, his boundless energy, moved over this desolate scene and in six days God created our world.

God knew that without light there could be no form of life. So on the very first day he commanded light to appear, dividing it from the total darkness which engulfed the blackened waters. In this way, he created day with its light when things could grow and people could work, and night in which everything could rest. God saw that it was all done perfectly.

But for life to survive, God recognized that a proper water supply was needed. Then on the second day God split up the waters – some to be in the sky to provide rain, the rest to be under the earth for springs and rivers. Again, everything was done just as it should have been.

Now it was time for earth to appear, crops to be sown, and trees planted. On the third day God first gathered together the waters which were still over all the earth into separate seas, allowing the continents to appear. And when he saw that the earth was ready for cultivation, God ordered it to produce every sort of grass, plants, and trees. And within them all, he provided seeds and pips so that every year they could renew themselves and continually produce more crops and fruit, all of which God made sure was very good.

But for there to be successful farming, there must be a regular pattern of cold and heat, rain and dry weather. Therefore, on the fourth day God created the sun to shine over the day and the moon to shine at night. He so organized their movements in the sky that he was able to provide the seasons of winter and summer, spring and autumn, as well as to order time with the hours, days, months, and years following each other in perfect rotation.

But life was not to be confined to the earth. The next day God commanded the seas to produce their shoals of fish and other marine animals from the smallest minnow to the largest whale. And on this fifth day he also filled the sky with flocks of birds. Both fish and birds delighted God, who told them to produce their young regularly so that the sea and air would always be full of them.

Then came the sixth day, on which it was earth's turn to be populated. God first made all the land mammals, both tame and wild, together with every kind of reptile and insect. Now God knew that everything was perfectly in place to enable him to create the human race. So God made men and women, commanding them to take charge of his creation for which they were now responsible, and urging them to have children so that the earth would always be looked after. He told them that, unlike the animals, whom they were to control, they were made in his image, that of all creatures they alone could communicate with him. He would listen to them and they must listen to him. Their task was to act like a mirror to reflect God's aims and ideas in maintaining his perfect world. He had entrusted it to their care. Everything depended on their proper management of the resources he had so generously given them. Finally, God pointed out that he had provided for humankind and the animals every kind of cereal, vegetable, and fruit for food so that in his creation there would be no blood shed. Humans and animals were designed to live together in perfect peace with each other.

But God provided one more day, the seventh, and on it God rested. He blessed that day, giving it to men and women as a holy day in which to enjoy themselves as God's friends freed from all daily work. Men and women knew that when they rested on the seventh day as God had rested they would always be sure of his blessing. No one, however powerful, could ever take that day away from them. Like everything else he had made on the last six days, it was God's gift, as secure as every other part of his creation. This was God's permanent sign of his everlasting commitment to his creation and the men and women for whom he had planned everything so carefully. His only concern was that they would have the faith to acknowledge him. He had given himself to them as their friend for ever: would there always be those who would respond?

That is how the world was made.

I have chosen the story of creation because it was written at a time of great loss of faith rather like our own. The Jews were in exile in heathen Babylon where many had rejected their God, believing that there was no hope for them in the future. Yet the story asserts that God will never let people go, no matter how disobedient they might be. God has pledged himself to his creation. It is men and women who decide their fate, not the God who created them and ever wills them to delight in all he has so richly provided.

The authors have taken over an ancient Babylonian story of creation in eight days, squashed it into six days (two things happen on days three and six) in order to use the seventh day for the creation of the sabbath, long practised by the Jews as a day of rest. The writers see the sabbath as an integral part of creation, like the sun and moon, the earth and sea, plants, animals and human beings. And since the only people in the world who keep the sabbath are the Jews, they must have been in God's mind at creation. They too have been fixed in the fabric of creation for all time. No foreign power could destroy them: only lack of faith in their own survival.

The authors then placed their reconstructed creation story before all the other already existing Bible stories to show that whatever mess the Jews had got into, God willed their salvation. Christians who have inherited the Hebrew Scriptures and their promises know from the first page of Scripture that God is for us. He loves his creation and will not abandon it. Only men and women can ruin its enjoyment by failing to accept what he has so graciously promised them, a promise he cannot revoke. Further, since all men and women are made in God's image for relationship with him, the promise is for all regardless of colour, race, or creed.

A hero for Israel

Monica Furlong

Bible reference
1 Samuel 16.1–17.58

In the days when Saul was king of Israel, he quarrelled with Samuel the prophet, the one who had chosen and anointed him as king. In many ways Saul had been a splendid king. He was a fine-looking man and a successful general — but then he had offended God by selfishly taking the spoils of war as his own possessions. Instead of sacrificing some of the best of the enemies' cattle, he kept them for his own herds. Although it was God who gave him victory, Saul secretly thought his success was due to his own cleverness. So Samuel rebuked him sternly, and Saul was very angry with the prophet. After that, Samuel went into hiding in fear for his life, and he grieved bitterly at losing the friendship of the king he had loved.

One day God told Samuel that it was time to stop grieving for his lost friend. Saul could no longer be king since he had become wicked and corrupt and was a bad example to his people. God had chosen a new king, and Samuel must travel to Bethlehem in order to seek him out. God told him to go to the house of an old man, Jesse, who had many sons, and anoint the one he would indicate. In order to keep what he was doing a secret, God told him to take a heifer with him, and when he got to Bethlehem, say that he had come there in order to offer a sacrifice. Then he must invite Jesse and his sons, among others, to attend the ceremony.

One by one, Jesse's fine sons passed before Samuel. When he saw the first, Eliab, tall and good-looking, Samuel thought he must be the future king, but God told him this was not the man. He thought the same with the next son, and the next, and kept feeling a quickening of excitement, but each time God told him "No", and reminded him that God does not see as human beings see. God can see into the heart. Finally, seven sons had passed before Samuel, and God had refused them all.

"Have you got any more sons?" Samuel asked Jesse.

"Well, there's David," said Jesse. "He's out looking after the sheep, but he's only a youngster."

"Fetch him!"

David arrived, out of breath from hurrying, and dirty from working with the sheep. He had a good face with beautiful eyes, and he was flushed from the sun and the open air. Samuel, who had great insight, felt at once that there was something unusual about him. And then he heard God's voice telling him that this was the future king of Israel. Samuel took his vial of oil, poured it upon the boy's head, and anointed him king.

David had a strong sense then of the spirit of God coming into him. Yet for a while nothing else very much seemed to change in David's life – he still continued to mind the sheep – and he found it hard to understand what Samuel's action could have meant.

Then he got a job at court. Saul had terrible moods, fits of black anger and depression, and his doctors suggested that what might help would be to have someone play soothing music to him at these times. David, although still so young, was known far and wide as a good musician who played the lyre (a sort of harp) very well, and so he was given an official job as the king's armour bearer, and, when Saul was in his black moods, he played music for him. Saul became very fond of him.

It was a difficult time for Israel. The Philistines, who wanted to destroy the Israelites, were massing huge armies against them and had invaded part of their territory. They were encamped upon one mountain, and the Israelites upon the opposite mountain, with a valley between them. Daily the Philistines taunted the Israelites to provoke them to battle, and the Israelites were afraid that if they fought they would lose. One of the Philistine torments was to send out a huge warrior, called Goliath, to stand in the valley and mock them. He was the biggest man any of them had ever seen, and he wore a huge bronze helmet on his head, a vast coat of mail, greaves of bronze upon his legs, and a javelin of bronze slung over his shoulder. In addition to the javelin, he carried a spear as big as a beam, tipped with iron, and a sword hung from his waist.

He roared out that he was the champion of the Philistines, and he challenged the Israelites to send out a champion against him. If Goliath won, he said, then the Israelites must become the slaves of the Philistines, and if the Israelites won then the Philistines would become the slaves of Israel. He struck terror into the Israelite camp, since no one felt they would stand a chance against the mighty Goliath. Not only would they certainly be killed but, in dying, they would deliver their people into the hands of the enemy.

David had gone home to Bethlehem to help his father with the sheep while this was going on, and had returned bearing food for his brothers, and a present of cheeses for the captain of his brothers' regiment. He found the Israelite army assembling for battle, and as he moved among the lines in search of his brothers he learned from the gossip of the soldiers the desperate situation in which Israel found itself. Then he heard Goliath come out and issue his challenge as he had done before. He saw how terrified everyone was by him, and heard the men discussing how Saul had promised that the man who killed him would be given great riches and would marry the king's daughter. But David was shocked that Goliath should dare to defy the armies of God, and said how shameful it was that Goliath should be allowed to mock God's people, and therefore God himself.

In time his words got back to Saul, who sent for him and questioned him. David was quite clear about what should be done.

"There is no need for anyone to be afraid. I, your servant, will go and fight with him!"

"That's impossible," said Saul. "You're only a boy!"

"Listen to me!" said David. "When I was looking after my father's sheep, one time the flock was attacked by a lion, and another time by a bear. I followed the lion, killed it, and took a young lamb out of its mouth. I fought single-handedly with the bear and killed him too. If the Lord saved my life when I was merely taking care of the sheep, surely he will defend me when I fight against the one who defies his armies!"

David's simple faith and courage moved Saul and somehow convinced him, though he also feared for him.

"Very well," he said. "Go, and the Lord be with you. You are a brave boy, and you shall wear my own special armour to protect you."

With Saul's help, David got dressed up in the king's magnificent armour – his bronze helmet, coat of mail and mighty sword – but when he tried to walk the suit of armour was so heavy that he could barely move.

"It's no good!" he said. "I'm not used to it. Let me make my own preparations."

He felt in his pouch and produced a simple sling – it was a weapon he used to scare the crows away from the young lambs – and then he went to the river and chose five smooth pebbles. He picked up his shepherd's crook.

"Now I'm ready," he said.

A huge crowd was assembled in the valley, Philistines on one side and Israelites on the other, but as the two champions strode out to meet one another there was an amazed silence. On the Philistine side there was a mighty warrior, armed to the teeth. On the Israelite side there was . . . a handsome young boy, apparently without any weapon at all. The Israelites groaned inwardly. What possible chance could this rash youngster have? The Philistines began to laugh.

Goliath, seeing David's simple crook, laughed louder than any.

"I'm a dog then, am I? Coming to drive me away with a stick, are you?"

Goliath cursed David and vowed that he would give his flesh to the birds of the air and the beasts of the field.

David announced to Goliath, "You come to me with sword and spear and javelin. I come to you in the name of the Lord of hosts, and today he will deliver you into my hand. Today you, and many of the host of the Philistines, will die!"

And David ran quickly towards Goliath, slipping a stone into his sling, which he flung with all the skill he had learned when he lived in the fields. The stone shot across the space between them and entered one of the few places on Goliath's armoured body that was not protected. It pierced his forehead, right between the eyes, and from there reached his brain and killed him. Goliath fell instantly to the ground.

David ran to his fallen enemy. He had no sword of his own, of course, but with difficulty he pulled Goliath's huge sword from its sheath, swung it high, and swept it down. He cut off the giant's head! Clutching it by the hair, he waved it aloft.

Terror seized the Philistines and they turned and fled, furiously pursued by the Israelites.

David returned to Jerusalem, carrying the head of Goliath, and Abner, the Israelite general, took him at once to Saul.

"Who are you, boy?" Saul asked him, suddenly seeing him with new eyes. "And what will you become?"

I first heard the story of David and Goliath at school when I was seven or eight, and I remember the excitement of it. I enjoyed the detail of David not being able to walk when he tried on Saul's armour. I was quite a fearful child, and liked stories about people who were brave because they seemed to make it easier for me to be brave. I think I learned something from this story about the way that believing in oneself, and one's cause, (and in David's case, in God) makes it possible to stand up to bullies – they can sometimes be overcome more easily than we expect. The story also points out that pride and conceit can bring about their own downfall. Goliath could scarcely be bothered with David, whereas David gave everything he had to the task in hand, and his youth, energy, and confidence succeeded. Stories don't always end so happily, but this one is oddly convincing.

The shepherd's watch

Sister Margaret Shepherd nds

Bible references
(1) Psalm 23
(2) Ezekiel 34
(3) Matthew 18.12–14 (Luke 15.3–7)
(4) John 10.14–15

The importance of caring, responsible leadership is clearly recognized in our world today. So, too, is the responsibility we all have to care for each other in our society, especially those most vulnerable, the "lost ones", the ones who have been hurt in some way or abandoned by our communities, whether the immediate community of the family, or the wider community.

One of the wonderful ways in which the writers of the Hebrew Scriptures spoke of God's loving care for his creation and especially for each one of us was to call God the "shepherd" of his people. And the behaviour of Israel's religious and political leaders, who had the duty to care for God's people, was measured against this yardstick. Jesus, too, makes use of this metaphor. The familiar theme of the shepherd in the Bible is a potent one which gives us much cause for reflection.

Among the poetry of the Bible, a favourite psalm is the one that begins "The Lord is my shepherd"[1]:

"I know for certain that God is the one who cares for me, looks after me, protects me. He will give me everything I need, everything that is good for me. Like a shepherd, he will make sure that I will be safe and secure and will make me calm when I am afraid or have been hurt. I have every confidence that God will lead me in the right way all through my life because he loves me and knows what is best for me.

"Sometimes life can be very hard and painful, even dangerous. Even at such moments I won't be afraid because I know that God, my loving shepherd, will be very close to me, guiding, protecting, and cherishing me.

"Even if I am surrounded by people who do not like me, who make life difficult for me, God will be very close to me and give me all that I need. He will show me how precious I am to him. He will shower me with special, wonderful gifts.

"With God as my shepherd, I am utterly sure that my life will be filled with love and forgiveness and tenderness. One day I shall live with God for ever."

Important leaders in the history of God's people, such as Abraham, Moses, and King David, were all shepherds at some time in their lives.

Jewish tradition speaks of Moses and David having to prove their ability to watch over sheep with loving care before God trusted them with the leadership of men and women. Once, it was said, a lamb escaped from Moses' flock, and when Moses left the others to follow it, he saw how it kept stopping to drink from the streams. So he realized how thirsty it had been and carried it tenderly back to the flock on his shoulder. God's response was, "As you took pity on a lamb and cared for it, Moses, I now know I can trust you to care for my people, Israel."

When later leaders, other kings, neglected the people and did not care for them properly, God's prophets, such as Ezekiel, spoke out strongly and sternly against them, calling them "shepherds" who had abandoned their "sheep"[2]:

"God told me to speak out against the 'shepherds' of my people. Instead of caring for them, all these so-called 'leaders' have cared only for themselves. They have been utterly selfish and have left everyone who needed help to fend for themselves — even the sick and the crippled, the children and those who are starving. This has to stop.

"So God has said that he himself will now be the 'shepherd' because he can no longer trust those who are meant to be in charge. He himself will look after his people and even go looking for those who have lost their way in life. He himself will make sure that they have food to eat and will make them well again if they are sick. God promises to make everyone safe and, in turn, asks them to stop being selfish and unkind to each other. To help them, he will give them a strong and good leader like King David. God will become personally involved with them, staying close to them, and making them secure. They will know that his blessings, his love, and his peace will always be with them. They are his very special people, the 'sheep of his flock', and he is their loving, faithful God, their 'shepherd'."

Jesus also spoke of God as a "shepherd" who loves and cares for his "sheep", his people. He told this story[3]:

"Let me ask you a question: Suppose a shepherd who owns a hundred sheep loses just one of them? What is he to do? Leave it to its own devices, not worrying about it? Let it get hurt or even killed? No, if he really cares, he leaves the ninety-nine sheep which are perfectly safe and goes looking for the one which is in danger and needs him. He searches everywhere. When he finds it, he will be absolutely delighted and want to celebrate!

"That's how God is with us. If we need him in a special way at certain times in our life, he will search for us, like the shepherd in the story, and bring us safely back, with love and tenderness and great rejoicing."

This is the way Jesus himself cared for others. He was a Jew who knew the Hebrew scriptures well, so he, too, spoke of himself as a "shepherd" who wanted the best for people[4]:

"I tell you, I am the 'good shepherd'. I care so much about you that I am even prepared to give my life for you. I will do anything for you, each one of you. I will protect you, love you, care for you. You are special and precious to me."

So the image of the shepherd, with its call to true leadership, is a very important one in both the Hebrew and the Christian scriptures and still means a great deal to Jews and Christians today who read those scriptures and pray with them.

On a personal note, my own surname is "Shepherd". It is now spelt in a variety of ways, but when I am asked the way I spell it, I usually reply, "As in the original!" I am proud that my own surname is "Shepherd": I have a great deal to live up to!

Twelve and missing

Heather Savini

Bible reference
Luke 2.41–52

T his trip was a milestone for our family. Having recently celebrated his twelfth birthday, our son was old enough to join us. It was a turning point for us as parents, too. Now that our son was becoming much more responsible, we could start to relax a little as we cut the ties and watched him launch himself into the big wide world. It made me feel so proud to see him becoming a man, though at times I regretted having to let go. I missed the mischievous grins and carefree spirit of childhood and the open sharing of joys and sorrows, tears and cuddles. But back to the journey . . .

We were off to Jerusalem to attend our chief religious festival of Pesach at the Temple. Just as our son was experiencing the freedom of adulthood, so our people remembered their freedom from slavery in Egypt and spent seven days thanking God for it. It was a challenging journey from Nazareth to Jerusalem but was made easier by the company of other pilgrims. We sang psalms as we walked and then at night, around camp fires, heard favourite stories of our ancestral heroes and heroines.

Jerusalem! What excitement had built up as we approached the city whose stones were alive with Israel's story! At last we saw God's special place, the Temple, dominating the city, with a plume of smoke rising on the skyline from the Temple sacrifices. It was so inspiring!

My son was completely awestruck by the sight. He wanted each detail to be explained to him. That was typical! Always curious to know and understand everything, he was constantly asking questions. Joe and I couldn't keep up with him. Many's the time we sent him to the rabbi to find his answers. I sometimes wondered where our son got his brains from! Naturally,

I suggested that the festival would be a wonderful opportunity to put all his questions about God to the rabbis in Jerusalem, and give us a bit of peace. "Surely they will have the answers," I said. "They spend long enough studying and arguing about all those deep matters."

Our boy had always taken religion seriously. But then we had often noticed he wasn't quite like other children. We had tried to treat him as a normal child – I mean, no one wants to know you if you are a bit different – but there was something special about him: he had a rare spirit.

It goes without saying that our son had a wonderful time at the festival. We didn't see a lot of him because he was off with his friends and listening to the rabbis in the temple court-yards. He needed some freedom, and we had to trust him to look after himself.

Of course, Pesach was over too quickly and we women set off home ahead of the men. I was unconcerned that my son was not with us. He knew I had left, and as a young man he would follow with his father. It was a shock when the men caught up with us at the end of a day's travelling, to discover my son wasn't with them! What a panic! We searched among friends and family – not a sign of him. There was nothing else for it but to retrace our steps right back to Jerusalem!

I didn't know what to think. It looked to me at first as if his new-found independence might have gone to his head. Then I began to worry that perhaps he was genuinely lost. One moment I was sorry for him and the next I was angry with him for causing all this anxiety and trouble. Joe and I fell to blaming each other:

"But, Joe, you knew he would be coming with you."

"Well, he was nowhere to be seen when we started out, so I assumed he was with you."

"Oh, didn't you ask his friends if they knew where he was?"

We spent two whole days searching every public place and alleyway in Jerusalem. We left descriptions of him and mess-ages for him, and as each day passed our anxiety grew. It was so out of character for him to act irresponsibly and that convinced me there really was something wrong. We wondered: would we ever see him again? Had he been harmed? Surely someone had spotted him!

In desperation, late on the third day, we checked the Temple courtyards yet again. What an immense relief to hear that familiar voice asking, "Rabbi, what do you think it really means?" I'd recognize that questioning tone anywhere! It was him. He was making quite an impression on the crowds with all his knowledge and wisdom.

But I was not impressed! I didn't want to show him up in public, but I was so relieved and exasperated at the same time that I found myself demanding, "Why have you treated us like this? Where have you been? Your father and I have been searching for you everywhere. We were worried to death."

I was staggered when he retorted, "Why did you come looking for me?" I thought a boy of his brainpower could have answered that one for himself! My patience was running out when he added, "Didn't you know I would be in my father's house?"

I was shocked. What did he mean? I didn't know whether he was being rude to us, trying to show off and impress those around us who were listening in, or whether there was something more in what he said. What was the relationship between him and God? Perhaps he meant that he would become a rabbi and teach others about God. Perhaps he was beginning to see what his destiny should be. I didn't know; I was utterly confused and Joe was, too.

Anyway, after three days of searching and worry, we were exhausted. Now that we had found him, we wanted to get home quickly. We had had enough! But then my anger dissolved, as he took my hand and squeezed it as if to say, "Sorry, mother, but can't you see I need to discover so much, and I had to make the most of my visit to understand what I need to be doing with my life?"

What a lot of thinking I did when we were safely home! Was my boy really so exceptional, or was it just because I was his mother that I thought he was? And what about his interest in God – was it genuine or would it be a passing phase? What had he got in mind? What had God got in mind for him? I was the one asking the questions, now! I decided to see if Elizabeth had had similar problems with John.

You can't help being concerned about what your children will make of themselves. I sensed something worthwhile would come from my son's life, though – already he had such sense of purpose, as if he knew he was destined for some high calling. Working with his father making ploughs and furniture wouldn't satisfy him for long.

It was many years later, that he did discover his destiny in life – seeking out others who had become lost, in so many different ways, and helping them to find their direction by living in God's way. And then it all came to a brutal end when he was executed so close to where we had found him that day.

At least it seemed like the end. Until on the third day . . .

I treasure this story because we are given an insight into Jesus' developing personality and his relationship with his parents. How true to life this "snapshot" appears in many respects, and yet how much larger than life in others! There is much here to reassure both young people and parents in their difficult roles and much to bewilder us in the enigmatic portrayal of Jesus.

The "Gentle Jesus, meek and mild" picture is challenged when we discover a rather self-centred, inconsiderate, and precocious boy! Jesus certainly has that determination of spirit that teenagers possess, appearing oblivious to his parents' responsibilities and anxiety. Here is a typical teenager, struggling with his self-identity, pondering career options and seeking to make sense of his world.

At the same time, Mary and Joseph wrestle with their parental role. Like most young people, Jesus resents his parents' interfering with his decisions and actions. They are rebuffed for not understanding and made to look and feel rather foolish. Most parents are similarly "shown up" by their teenage offspring, for fussing unnecessarily. Likewise, they have trusted their teenage children and then been let down.

Parents worry about the future of their offspring. Jesus is to cause his family a lot of anxiety and heartache, so firm is his growing awareness of a special destiny that awaits him. But his family do not seem to be a party to his thoughts and we sense a growing gulf between what they comprehend and what Jesus is able to disclose to them. How often must Mary, as a responsible parent, have intervened as she did in Jerusalem and been left confounded and even rejected? I guess she and Elizabeth would spend hours in discussion, proud of their sons, yet puzzled about where their destinies would lead them.

However much Mary and Joseph might have anticipated a less than normal childhood for Jesus, and however much they grasped about their son's true identity, theirs was a daunting responsibility! Having the "son of God" as your own son was a high calling indeed!

On this family trip to Jerusalem, as in his birth records, the mystery and the paradox of the boy Jesus are revealed. We glimpse human life converging with the Godhead in the mystery of the Incarnation.

A new day

Fay Sampson

Bible reference
John 21.1–19

It was all over. Us striding into Jerusalem with Jesus riding a donkey and the crowd going mad with palm branches. That last supper, when Jesus washed our feet and gave us bread and wine. The awful moment in the olive orchard, Jesus down on his knees praying his heart out, and then the torchlight and soldiers, and Judas stepping out of the darkness to kiss him. The others ran. Not me. I followed, right to the High Priest's house. Then they shut the door in my face and I was left in the yard. I'll never forget his face when they brought him out, tied up, a prisoner. That was the last time I saw Jesus alive.

They crucified him. As if he was a murderer. John and some of the women saw him put in a tomb. I couldn't bear to watch. All that life, laughter, love, gone for ever. And I'd thought he was the Son of God. I went back to Mark's house and hid myself.

No, I haven't told you the whole truth. It was worse than that.

He'd warned us this was going to happen, only we couldn't take it in. We were so sure he was going to bring in the Kingdom of Heaven. I told Jesus off for talking about getting himself killed. That wasn't in my plans. It was an awful thing when I realized he'd been telling us the truth.

Even then, I wouldn't give up. He told us we'd all run away and leave him. Of course, we all argued that we wouldn't. I shouted louder than anybody else. He knew me better. He always saw me more clearly than I could see myself.

"You will, Peter. Three times you'll swear you never knew me, before cock-crow tomorrow."

I wish I didn't have to tell you. Inside the High Priest's house, Jesus was on trial for his life. And I was outside, trying to keep warm by their fire in the low, small hours of the morning. I tried not to be noticed, but they spotted my accent. A girl blurted out, "Didn't I see you with that Jesus they're going to hang? You're from up north too. Galilee."

And without stopping to think, I shouted, "I've never met the man."

How could I have said that? Never met Jesus? When he loved me, deeper than my own mother or father or wife or child? And once I'd lied, I couldn't go back on it. Three times I said it. They all heard me.

Just as it was getting light, they dragged Jesus out. I saw his face. He looked as lonely as if he hadn't a friend in the world. They hauled him past me and he looked straight at me. Me, that swore I was his friend. And then the cock crowed.

I couldn't stop crying when I heard he was dead. I've always prided myself on being the big, tough fisherman. Only now I knew I was nothing. It was the women who were the tough ones. They stood by the cross and watched him die.

They were the ones who saw him first. It was the third day. Some women had gone to the tomb with fresh herbs and spices, to see to his body properly now the Sabbath was over. John and I stayed indoors, sunk in gloom. The women came racing back.

"He's gone! Somebody's taken him!"

We dashed out to the tomb where they'd put him. The big stone in front was rolled away. John stood in the doorway, staring, as though something had happened he couldn't believe. I pushed past him and went right in. And there was the oddest thing. Jesus' body was gone. But the cloths the women had wrapped him in were still there.

I didn't understand, not even when Mary Magdalene came with a face like sunshine, crying how he'd met her, there in the garden.

And then he appeared. To us. We were all together in the house. It really was him, the living Jesus we'd known. Only . . . I can't explain this, but I knew, more certainly than I ever had before, that I'd met the Son of God.

We saw him again. And then, nothing. The women had said there'd been a message to tell me he'd be going ahead to Galilee. So I went home.

There were seven of us on the beach that night. We were pretty low. The excitement was over. We didn't really know what to do next. I'd always thought of myself as leader of the twelve. But I wasn't fit. Three times I betrayed Jesus the night they arrested him. John was the quieter one, but he was the only man of the apostles who stayed by the cross with the women.

I'd had enough.

"I'm going fishing," I said. "Who's coming?"

We launched the boat, headed for deep water and slung the gear over the side. We were out of luck. It was still the same, sitting around in the dark, with nothing happening. It was a hot night. We were tired and we'd stopped talking.

The sky was just starting to show light over the hills. It was the time of day I found it hardest to bear now, waiting for the cock to crow.

Voices travel a long way over water. We heard someone call to us, "Have you got any fish?" There was a light on the beach, but we couldn't make out who was standing there.

"No," we shouted back.

"Throw your net out to starboard."

Well, I was captain of this fishing boat. I wasn't having some landlubber teach me my job. Then John caught hold of my arm. He senses things sometimes, quicker than I do.

"Do what he says."

We shifted all the gear from one side to the other and threw out the big net again. And next instant, it was so full of fish we couldn't haul it in.

"It's him!" John breathed.

I didn't need telling twice. I grabbed the tunic I'd stripped off for work and jumped overboard.

We were only a hundred metres off shore. I headed for the fire on the beach, and the man standing beside it. I swam till my feet touched stones and I staggered ashore.

It was Jesus. And what do you think he was doing? He'd made a charcoal fire. And he was grilling fish over it. There was bread ready.

The Son of God. Crucified. Risen from the dead. Cooking breakfast on the beach. For us.

"Bring some of your fish," he told me. So I set to and hauled the net on shore, where they'd just landed it.

"Breakfast's ready."

Imagine the seven of us, sitting round the fire with Jesus, eating fresh fish and new-baked bread, and watching the sun come up over the Sea of Galilee.

I could have sat by the lakeside for ever sharing that meal. But Jesus never lets you sit still for too long. He had work for me. We walked along the shore.

Presently he said, "Simon, John's son." That was my old name, before I met him and he nicknamed me Peter the Rock. "Do you love me more than the rest?"

I shouted out quick at that, as I usually did. "You know I do."

He looked at me very straight and stern. "Feed my lambs."

A few minutes later he asked me, "Simon, do you love me?"

That hurt. I'd shouted it loud enough. He didn't need to ask twice, did he? Then I remembered the night when he was on trial for his life. My voice dropped a bit lower.

"Lord, you know I love you."

There was a bit of a sad smile around his mouth. "Look after my sheep."

We walked on, and there was only the sound of our feet on the stones and the waves lapping.

"Do you really love me?"

I hung my head. I knew why he had to ask me a third time. What had I got to boast about? I muttered so low he must have had a job hearing me.

"Lord, you know me. You know how much I love you."

And he put his arm round my shoulders and the laughter came back to his eyes, like it always used to.

"Feed my sheep. And follow me."

So I knew he'd forgiven me.

And when he hugged me, I could smell woodsmoke and fried fish.

This story astonishes and delights me. The appearance of the risen Christ is so unexpected. A beach barbecue, with Jesus as breakfast cook?

God is often pictured as an emperor: the crown, the throne, a glittering court.

The evening he was arrested, Jesus tied an apron round him, went down on his knees and washed the dust off his followers' feet, like a low-paid servant. Now he has been crucified, and risen with life everlasting. *And he is still the same.*

This is the Son of God who is up before sunrise, cooking our breakfast on the beach.

Teaching the Bible

Biblos is a research project based at the University
of Exeter School of Education. It works in schools in
Devon and London (Ealing) in Key Stages 2 and 3 (ages 7 to
13). In the UK, where society appears to be largely secular
or plural (or both!) many schools have given up teaching
the Bible. They can't see how to do it in an interesting
way and they are sometimes afraid that in a multi-faith
school teaching the Bible might cause problems. Biblos
worked from a different starting point: the awareness
that what was commonly known as "the Bible" contains
the sacred writings of two religions, Judaism and Christianity, and deals with some of the prophets in a third
religion, Islam. Parts of both Testaments have themselves
been referred to or been influenced by other religions:
Canaanite, Babylonian, Greek, Roman and so on. It is
already a text with multi-religious implications.

In consultation with scholars from different faith
communities, the Biblos team identified three key
concepts in the Bible that "bridge" into the life of all
humankind: Destiny, Vulnerability and Encounter. Ways
of dealing with these concepts are being explored in the
classroom in our partner schools. Published curriculum

materials available for all schools are planned, alongside a research report which will explain how and why we took this particular approach. This book is one off-spin of the research project.

Biblos address:
The Biblos Project,
School of Education,
University of Exeter,
Heavitree Road,
Exeter
EX1 2LU

Biblos acknowledges with thanks its financial sponsors:

All Saints Educational Charity
Devon LEA
Ealing LEA
The Foundation of St Matthias
The London Bible House Fund
The St Luke's College Foundation Trust

Bible Societies

Bible Societies exist to provide resources for Bible distribution and use. The United Bible Societies is a world-wide fellowship of National Bible Societies working in more than 180 countries. Their aim is to reach all people with the Bible or some part of it in a language they can understand and at a price they can afford. Around 600 million Scriptures are distributed by these Societies every year. You are invited to share in this work by your prayers and gifts. The Bible Society in your country will be very happy to provide details of its activity.